CLARISSA
AND THE
COUNTRYMAN

Also by Clarissa Dickson Wright:

The Haggis: a Little History
Food
Hieland Foodie: A Scottish Culinary Voyage with Clarissa

with Jennifer Paterson
Two Fat Ladies
Two Fat Ladies Ride Again
Two Fat Ladies: Full Throttle
Two Fat Ladies: Obsessions

CLARISSA
AND THE
COUNTRYMAN

CLARISSA DICKSON WRIGHT
AND JOHNNY SCOTT

HEADLINE

In memory of Walter

FIRST PUBLISHED IN 2000 BY HEADLINE BOOK PUBLISHING
BY ARRANGEMENT WITH THE BBC
THE BBC LOGO IS A TRADEMARK OF THE BRITISH BROADCASTING CORPORATION
AND IS USED UNDER LICENCE
BBC LOGO © BBC 1996

10 9 8 7 6 5 4 3 2 1

BRITISH LIBRARY CATALOGUING IN PUBLICATION DATA IS AVAILABLE FROM THE BRITISH LIBRARY

ISBN 0-7472-3247-4

DESIGNED BY DESIGN PRINCIPALS, WARMINSTER

PRINTED AND BOUND IN GREAT BRITAIN BY BUTLER AND TANNER LTD, FROME, SOMERSET

HEADLINE BOOK PUBLISHING
A DIVISION OF HODDER HEADLINE
338 EUSTON ROAD
LONDON NW1 3BH

WWW.HEADLINE.CO.UK
WWW.HODDERHEADLINE.COM

CONTENTS

We took advantage of Clarissa's being a Freeman of the City of London to drive sheep over London Bridge

INTRODUCTION

We have both put a great deal of time, effort and energy into making the television programmes and writing this book because we believe passionately in a way of life which is under threat from misunderstanding, misconception and bureaucratic interference. That energy will have been in vain if those of you who are Townies, or who do not understand the points we are trying to make, do not read this book with an open mind and a willingness to 'listen to us'.

In Johnny, the countryside is bred in the bone and he was born knowing far more than I shall ever learn. But for me it is a learnt experience and therefore one that is available to all of you. We hope that you will not allow brainwashing, preconditioning or ignorance to affect your reading of this book. For those of you who are of the country, we trust that you will find entertainment, enjoyment and even new information herein.

We would like to thank BASC, the Countryside Alliance and all our friends, both old and new, whose help has made this venture possible. We'd also like to thank Jane Root for having the vision to commission the television programmes, and the BBC, both in England and Scotland, for being willing to learn and join in the adventure, for that is what it has been for both of us.

We would also like to thank Heather Holden-Brown in particular, and Headline Books in general, for the enthusiasm and encouragement they have given us.

It is indicative of the divide between town and country that Angela Mackworth-Young, our long-suffering Townie editor, thought it necessary to advise the inclusion of a glossary of country terms which you will find in the back of this book. She prevented us, forcefully, from being facetious.

Clarissa Dickson Wright
and
Johnny Scott

October 2000

A MEET IN CHILDHOOD

C I was born a Townie on 24 June 1947, in the London Clinic, and raised all the days of my childhood in a large house encircled by its own garden in St John's Wood. There are times when I feel the urban slurry in my soul still: when I worked on a pheasant farm and a dog fox got in and took the heads off 600 poults in one night I would gladly have exterminated every fox in the British Isles but, as Johnny says, what would we do in the winter?

We were not totally urbanized – my father shot – although all I ever knew about it were the fruits of his labours either hanging in the game larder or tasting delicious. He was, I believe, a good shot and used also to go to Bisley. I went with him once and was amazed at the complexity of the set-up, a whole town of clapboard bungalows with dining-halls *et al* just for competitive rifle shooting.

My mother and my sister Heather hunted; they both rode side-saddle and looked wonderfully elegant. My mother's favourite story was how, when staying with the Dundonalds in Ireland, she took her first bank. Irish banks are huge, imposing edifices and it is necessary for the horse to leap to the top, change feet and jump off the other side. My mother had heard tell of all the necessary techniques and was going neck or nothing for the bank when her host came up alongside her shouting, 'Pull up. He's never topped a bank before.' My mother's blood was up and, in truth, I suspect the horse had taken hold, so they took the bank like a good 'un and flew off the other side with perfection, earning admiration and repeat invitations from her hosts.

On the same occasion my father had been given a horse that was hobdayed: it carted him. He could only halt it by leaning down and placing a hand over the hole, which stopped it dead every time. I never saw my father on a horse, though I believe he was quite competent but no more. My maternal grandmother was a formidable horsewoman and even used to pig-stick side-saddle. She looked very well in riding kit and knew it, and the family albums mostly show her in breeches and boots, surrounded by her salukis and terriers, talking to a horse, usually without her side-saddle skirt.

These were the tales of my childhood. As you can see riding, and indeed hunting, were a female activity in my home, so it was with great excitement that I went off to learn to ride. Nobody had told me that it would be difficult, painful and frustrating but oh so compulsive.

Country children have ponies or friends with ponies: the Thelwell child is a country child. You grab your bridle after breakfast and rush off to ride, and then spend happy hours mucking out, rubbing down, curry-combing, plaiting, bandaging and simply talking to your pony. You acquire your confidence by falling off a succession of ponies, being hit by low branches and running back to mummy crying, 'My silly old collar-bone's bust', only to be met with the stern words, 'Have you seen to your pony, darling?' An animal teaches responsibility and consideration.

Escape from London

Town children go to riding schools: you get dressed up in the right clothes and go by car to Rotten Row or Richmond Park. In the country you don't have to be well off to ride; in the town it is expensive. I went to Richard Stillwell, who coached the British Olympic team, and it was a forty-minute drive to Windsor Park (one hour actually, if you obeyed the speed limit, which my mother never did). Like most children's first pony mine, called Aster, was a fat teddy bear and drumming my heels into her flanks only produced a grudging canter.

I have an early memory of sitting on my backside in the mud as my sister Heather, superlatively elegant on her liver-chestnut hunter, Sam Brown, Dick Stillwell on a big bay and Heather's friend, Alekki, on a pretty grey Arab with a long flowing tail, all cantered away from me against the backdrop of Windsor Castle. Beastly Aster cropped the grass as if I didn't exist. This incident made such an impression on me that I wrote a poem about it. After riding there was no mucking out, no grooming, none of the things that a country child would have done, just straight into my mother's Bristol and home for a bath.

Hunting was different. If, for instance, you hunted with the Garth and South Berks you got up early, drove down and your horse was boxed over. But for anything further away you went and stayed with friends and, if the meet was more than an hour from Windsor, they mounted you. An expensive little exercise as you can see, and one that doesn't immerse you in the community and the real spirit of the Hunt.

It is thanks to my friend Christine that I really spent time in the country. She was my best friend at school and remains so to this day. My own home life was unhappy and I was so much the youngest that I was quite alone. Christine – an object of envy to me – lived with her seven brothers and sisters in a sprawling house in the village of Selmeston in East Sussex. It was here that I spent every minute I could – playing in the hay, falling into ditches and getting kicked or dumped by Misty, the foul-tempered Welsh mountain pony. It was my idea of heaven. I found an old diary in which I had written, aged fifteen, that this was my favourite place on earth – and I a girl who had been round the world and stayed at some of the most luxurious places on the planet.

I must have been eleven when I first met Johnny. His father was very much the squire in the best old-fashioned sense, and they lived in the next village to Selmeston. Johnny was an amazingly scruffy small boy with an unruly crop of red gold curls; his jerseys were always ripped and his shorts' pockets (he denies the shorts but I have photographic evidence) bulged with the sorts of things small boys love. It seemed to me he was never without his ferret, which lived in his shirt and with which he would alarm the small girls of the neighbourhood. It didn't half pong and it generously bestowed its fragrance on its owner! Apart from Johnny's ferret there was his terrier, a potentially enchanting Jack Russell that went everywhere with him and competed with the ferret to be carried inside his jacket. He confessed recently that he had found a childhood photo album which consisted of twenty-five photos of ferrets and twenty-five of terriers and nothing else!

Johnny the scruffy small boy

Johnny had a wonderful arrogance about him and seemed infinitely superior, largely due to the fact that he could, and would, ride anything. Johnny is a natural horseman. When we were filming the hunting programme (see Chapter Five), I was worried that he would be going out in some of the most dangerous country on a hireling that he had never even had the chance to try out, let alone ride to hounds. This anxiety was further exacerbated by Johnny's quiet demeanour at breakfast, which I discovered later was due to distaste for his new hard hat and not apprehension. I needn't have worried: such skills don't leave you.

Johnny grew into a elegant, graceful and wild young man with all the attributes of a countryman. The county resounded with his escapades, the glory of his being brakeman for the British bob-sleigh team, and of his hunting with his long hair – it was the Sixties – tucked up under his hat. His ruddy curls were often spotted shinning up a national monument, or the drainpipe to some lady's chamber. But the years rolled by and Johnny came less often to Sussex, and to the Yew Tree at Chalvington, that centre of village life.

Six years ago I moved to Scotland and there was Johnny: his curls undimmed and untamed, his humour as sharp, and the unceasing quest for knowledge and information that had

About to unload stag from a garron

drawn us together in the first place still intact – awfully relentless Johnny. The thing about old friends is you pick up where you left off, as if time has stood still.

How frightfully mundane to have been born in the London Clinic. I, on the other hand, was born at home, Hamsland Holt in Sussex, during the great storm of 1948. My father had to carry the midwife on his back, in through the snowdrifts. A surviving memento of the occasion is in my filing cabinet, an envelope inscribed: 'J. Scott, His Caul, 24 February 1948'. Shortly after my birth we moved to Scarletts Farm in that lovely wooded, undulating part of the Kent and Sussex border. It was an enchanting place with a lake and a weir, four cottages, a watermill, an oast house and a beautiful timbered Elizabethan house, large enough for a nursery wing to contain my sister and me.

It is really here that my childhood memories start: the pale green colour of the nursery walls, the succession of nannies – the least agreeable of whom I succeeded in knocking unconscious by rolling a toy tractor under her foot. I can still hear the lovely sound of her squawk, and the thud as she hit the floor. I remember the smell of my mother's scent when she came to kiss me goodnight, and the faces of the people who worked for my father: Bill Akehurst, the horseman,

Meet of the Southdown Hounds at Selmeston

Matt, the cowman, and Joe Botting, the pigman, who took me ferreting; Mrs Rogers, who worked in the house, and her father, who had lost both feet in the First World War and got about on leather-covered kneepads.

There were cart-horses, hunters and an evil-tempered grey pony called Twilight on whom I hunted for the first time, aged five, led on foot by my perspiring father. A succession of hound puppies spring to mind. Our local Hunt always presented puppy walkers with silver teaspoons at the annual puppy show. A few of these have survived, engraved with their names and the year they were with us: Outcast and Harmony 1952; Dexter and Melody 1954; Furrier and Falcon 1955.

The smell of boot polish and Rangoon oil always conjures up pictures of the boot-room, with gleaming rows of my parents' hunting boots, and a gun-room where the terriers had their beds: Tiger, Tarka and Tweedle, taciturn Sealyham-crosses that were my father's pride and joy. They were proper working terriers, bred for the job. I learnt my first lessons in the treatment of animals from them. Their master's son I may have been, but that didn't mean they were going to tolerate any liberties.

We moved to Eckington Manor, a red-brick Queen Anne house with more productive farmland overlooking the church in the village of Ripe, when I was six. It was here that the parameters of my life began to become apparent. The family had moved south from Northumberland at the turn of the century, but kept the land and forestry. There were other business interests as well in the north, and once a month my father would go up there, sometimes taking me with him. In the summer we might go as a family, breaking the journey to the Spey when my parents went up there to fish.

My mother's parents lived on the Ashdown Forest in a house where the extensive cellars and attics were an Aladdin's cave to a small boy. There were trunks filled with old uniforms, bundles of native weaponry, assegais, knobkerries and Burmese kris, through which I spent hours rummaging happily. My father's father lived near Ardingly and his chauffeur, Jack Davidson, who had started with us as my great-grandmother's coachman, held me riveted with stories of my grandfather racing at Brooklands in the early days of motor-racing.

This is the age when a child learns to love and respect wildlife. It is the time when you are taught about the breeding seasons and how hedges and woodland are managed for wildlife, and as my sister and I grew older we became more involved in the adult world. Ponies got bigger and more manageable and we joined my father and the grooms on morning exercise. Soon we were hunting off the leading rein and being taught the difference between good scenting days and bad; how a huntsman pits his skill and knowledge against one of the most cunning animals on earth. We learnt how nature helps the huntsman judge the line a fox may be taking – birds flock, and livestock bunch as a fox passes by them trying to check hounds by muddling the scent. We learnt the manners of the hunting field and the courtesies of the countryside. We were on other people's land by their invitation, and that of the Master: his Hunt Servants had a job to do and we were spectators. We learned that the only person hunting the fox was the Huntsman. The field were there because of their love of horses and riding, and of the unexpected challenges provided by the line a hunted fox takes across country. That and the enjoyment they get from watching hounds work.

Field sports were not seen in isolation in those days. They were, and still are, the catalyst that binds many country communities together. As a child I grew up at ease with country people. Through hunting I met the farmers over whose land we hunted, and the people who worked for them. I saw them at markets and in the local town. Relations, who lived in various parts of the country, were all involved in field sports and by association I knew the same people they knew. Several cousins and all my godparents were MFHs (Masters of Foxhounds). Those involved in hunting all know each other. It gave me a wonderful feeling of security knowing that I had connections with countrymen throughout Britain. If life at school became particularly bloody, I would console myself with the thought that, when it finally became unbearable, a safe haven lay in the nearest Hunt kennels.

It was an idyllic childhood, interrupted only by unpleasant periods at boarding school. We hunted and shot through the winter, fished in the early summer and went down to the West Country to stag-hunt in August. I had a terrier of my own, and I always had ferrets. In a moment of filial devotion I christened a little polecat jill, the ferret to whom I was most attached, Diana. Prophetically, my ferrets were used in one of the *Out of Town* programmes presented by Jack Hargreaves. Life seemed to be so rock steady.

My father, a man of enormous energy, was able to do what he saw to be his duty to the countryside. Apart from his farming and business interests in the north he was a JP and a DL. On the Hunt committee, actively involved in the pony club and each year he designed and built the hunter-trial course. President of the village cricket team and Chairman of the Parish Council. Instrumental in opening up a continual bridleway from where we lived in Sussex to Salisbury. Regenerated the local bell-ringing team and rang himself. Even had me at it for a bit. Bred and showed hunters and eventers, and went everywhere with a pack of terriers. And, in her own quiet way, my mother was deeply committed to her involvement with the church and the welfare of the village.

But great changes were afoot. The farms in Northumberland were sold and the proceeds invested badly. I left school and went away to South Africa, Australia and New Zealand for a couple of years. I arrived back in time to see the brick dust settle and watch the black cloud of Lloyds' losses gathering on the horizon. Uncertain what to do now that the farms were gone, I was persuaded to try the City, a way of life to which I was totally unsuited and could never settle. There were no regrets when I left, on either side, and with a wife in tow I enrolled on the sheep course at the Northumberland College of Agriculture which specialized, in part, in marginal and hill farming. With limited funds, farms were as difficult to come by then as they are now, and despite the depression, I eventually found a partnership in a hill farm on the Lammermuirs. By and large we have been very happy, and we could not have brought up our family in a more beautiful or more healthy situation. Until he was made redundant by the now ubiquitous quad-bike, I did all my herding on a garron. I had my sheepdogs, terriers and ferrets.

Hill farming fascinates me: the sheep are practically wild animals and I love the broad perspective, the coming and going of the migratory birds, the chuckle of the grouse and nature's gentle rhythm. My participation in field sports was by now pretty limited, a bit of ferreting, the occasional day's shooting and a little fishing. As my children grew older, we acquired a New Forest pony of questionable age and my daughter was taught to ride. When my son was seven he was given a .410 and, rather earlier than I had intended, I began to teach him to shoot. I experienced the same exquisite pleasure in his wide-eyed excitement, and gradual acquisition of knowledge and love of the countryside, that my own father must have had when he taught me.

It is a most wonderful privilege, passing on this priceless gift of ours. My only sadness is that we live outside hunting country. I could not have afforded to hunt any more anyway, but you do not have to hunt to be involved or part of it. The other day I was talking about this to Mr Lowe of Stewart Christie, the Edinburgh tailor who lives in hunting country. He produced a classic example: 'You know old Mrs X who hunts with us? She died early yesterday morning. By eight o'clock last night I bet you at least two hundred people knew she was dead.'

I miss living in a community whose hub is generated by a Hunt: the foot followers' dinners, quiz nights, jumble sales, auctions, point-to-points, hunter trials and puppy shows – all the contact and communication that had been such a large part of the first thirty years of my life.

My first recollection of Clarissa was at one of those semi-formal children's parties that someone's parents had gone to enormous trouble to lay on, and which I hated more than I can describe. Recently shorn and forced into a suit, I would spend these frightful events stoically resisting attempts to make me join in the parent-organized dancing. Inevitably, try as I might, an incident would occur for which there would be recriminations when I got home.

I have a mental picture of a dining-room filled with groups of children eating at different tables. Across the room I could see Fat-Boy Rory Hudson wearing, of all things, a red bow-tie. Supremely self-confident and with his lank dark hair parted in the middle, the sight of him infuriated me. Earlier in the evening he had sneeringly dismissed ferreting as an occupation for farm labourers. On the spur of the moment I hurled a bread roll at him and, as it flew through the air, the strange girl from London opposite me rose to watch its trajectory.

'Bull's-eye!' she shouted with glee, her eyes wide with excitement. 'Slap in his soup. Well done! Now watch this.'

With incredible speed she snatched up a knife and, using the blade, indiscriminately fired a dish of butter pats at the surrounding tables. I was speechless with admiration. In the ensuing chaos, and through a hail of assorted foodstuffs, I somehow managed to shake her hand.

Clarissa came to stay with schoolfriends in a neighbouring village most holidays and, although the kaleidoscope of memories is pretty indistinct after forty years, her sheer energy, joy in life, love of people and her ability to bring out the best in others are what stick in the mind. There was a determination then, undiminished today, that life should not just be fun but terrific fun. For Clarissa, the countryside was a Pandora's box of wonder, fascination and memories to be taken home and treasured in London.

After school our paths crossed infrequently. There was a chance meeting in the City, or an invitation to some party in an obscure part of London. The well-remembered laugh would rise from the depths of a nightclub and she would include me in some crazy venture as dawn broke. By then, Clarissa was a rising star in the legal firmament, whose contacts had become worldwide. She had been everywhere and knew everyone. Mention Tehran and you would be told not to go there until July when Yusef's melons were at their best: third stall on your left as you go down the bazaar towards the mosque. Give him my love. Going to Moscow? Be sure to look up Boris Litzinoff, Minister of Inland Fisheries, and tell him to put less salt in the caviar. Last year's batch was inedible. Taking the children to Blackpool? Have a word with the man who runs the big dipper, his wife is second cousin of my mother's maid, Emily. He'll give you a dead cert for the National. Her generosity and kindness were legendary and all too often, 'Send me the bill' became her byword.

But life can be very cruel. By the mid-Eighties I came south only infrequently and I hadn't seen her for years. One morning I bumped into her outside the Yew Tree in Chalvington. The hoot of welcome was defiantly still the same, but the pain and anguish in her eyes confirmed the rumours far more than the shabby clothes. There was a long moment of recognition before she changed the subject and looked away. Rummaging in a pocket she produced her snuffbox, the hallmark of her days as a barrister.

'Look, look,' she said, proffering it with a trembling hand. 'Your favourite, Fribourg's Santo Domingo. This is the last of it. Have some.'

Those who knew her then wonder that she survived. She did, thank God, and, in February 1994, she moved to Scotland. This was the old Clarissa, altered in some respects, but with the same ability to make others see the best of their situations and enjoy life through her sheer energy, enthusiasm and irrepressible good humour. Desperately short of cash she still managed, somehow, to give dinner parties where the finest food, chosen with infinite care, was cooked in conditions of incredible chaos.

The series of circumstances that eventually led to the making of the television programmes started in 1994. Guy Ross-Lowe, who has been a friend since dame school, rang up one day with an idea. Guy had been Joint Master of the Cheshire and had become very fond of Johnnie O'Shea, the huntsman, a terrific character and one of the most famous huntsmen of his generation. I had known Johnnie for some years and acquired a couple of really topping terriers from him. After forty-one years in Hunt Service and twenty-five seasons with the Cheshire, Johnnie was retiring. Among others, Guy was deeply concerned that Johnnie would now become a rudderless ship. Lord Leverhulme had already made him an honorary member of the Altcar Coursing Club, and Guy had the inspiration of getting several of us to put up some money to buy Johnnie a greyhound pup and form a coursing syndicate. I was dead keen. Years ago I had gone coursing with the Jack Jones Coursing Club on the Romney Marshes and loved it. Negotiations then took place between Johnnie and his great crony in Ireland, Mickey Flanagan. Mickey had been Kennel Huntsman of the Tipperary and was now a greyhound breeder and luminary in the coursing world. After some confusion, two four-month-old pups arrived and the Cholmondeley Coursing Club was up and running.

There followed a period of intense excitement and the sheer joy in pride of ownership, with frequent visits to stay with Guy and Carolyn to see the puppies as they grew and filled out under Johnnie's care. There were splendid club dinners at the Cholmondeley Arms, Guy and Carolyn's pub, with endless speculation and discussion about anticipated future triumphs. I started poppng down to Northumberland whenever the Coquetdale had meetings and, in September 1996, we had our first runner at the Altcar meeting.

After the 1997 Waterloo Cup, the syndicate discovered that certain members, carried away by the excitement of the event, had agreed to buy two more puppies off Mickey Flanagan. To keep the syndicate's continuity intact we actually needed young dogs coming on, but it meant the syndicate had to expand to cover costs. The success of *Two Fat Ladies* had brought about a change in Clarissa's fortunes and she leapt at the opportunity of joining us when I suggested it.

In May 1997 the Socialists came to power. They had reputedly accepted £1 million from IFAW, the International Fund for Animal Welfare, to put a Bill to ban hunting before parliament. As a prime minister, Blair will be remembered as the man who united the countryside and showed us the power of public demonstration. On 10 July 1997, in between gathering and shearing, Clarissa, Mary, my wife, our son and I took the train to King's Cross for the first of these, the Hyde Park Rally. It was an historic day, the first of many to come.

C I went with Johnny and his family and Isabel, who runs my shop (and would hunt six days a week given half a chance. Her father hunted seven: they do in Ireland) on the train from Dunbar on a journey that was to change our lives. I stood in Hyde Park surrounded by friends, some of whom I had not seen for many years, and wept at my old friend Baroness Mallalieu's speech. I am not one for causes, and too lame and lazy for marches, but I vowed that day that I should not 'Cease from mental fight, nor shall my sword sleep in my hand,' until we had won. I knew that I might be throwing away a successful career and

Peaceful, for the moment

risking a loss of popularity, but I believe in the British ability to respect personal freedoms and I trust I am right. This vow saw me marching again in London with 450,000 others; took me on *Question Time* as the voice of the Countryside Alliance; and saw me standing before a crowd of 20,000 at the Newcastle rally holding up a banner of Adolph Hitler that Isabel had made (he was the last man to ban fox-hunting in 1932). Hitler's chilling words were, 'Henceforth the only killing in this country will be done by professional butchers'. Ruthless ambition and the search for cheap votes killed a lot of people.

Since the start of the Foster Bill the countryside has organized a series of marches and rallies, all of which have been very well attended. The first rally in Hyde Park was organized by the Hunts, and their supporters, with groups marching all the way from the four corners of the United Kingdom and swelling with added walkers as they went. Thereafter there was the great London march, and marches and rallies in Newcastle, Birmingham, Wales and Inverness, Exeter and Bournemouth. The marches were all peaceful, good-humoured, tidy and quick. We were simply there to be counted and, for the most part, the marches didn't attract the media attention they should have. Today most of us want something more radical and are only held in check by our leaders, whom we trust. The Welsh blocked the Severn Bridge recently, by marching across it. We have shouted 'Listen to us' and 'Freedom means choice', but the countryside is becoming tired of being ignored and there is a militant spirit abroad. When reason and lawyers are done, one remembers that Cromwell was a country squire who came to London with his friends on heavy horses! Let's watch what Mr Blair will do.

There are two things I remember most about that first march. One was the mounted police forces, picketed under the trees along Birdcage Walk, the police dozing in the shade. The other was an enormous bearded man leaping onto the train at Berwick. He was a shepherd from somewhere on the Cheviot who had missed his subsidized bus from Wooler. He'd driven through the mist to Berwick and spent all his cash on the train ticket. He had lost his mates, was now penniless and had never been on a train before nor anywhere further south than Newcastle. But one way or another he was determined to be at the rally. This is the sort of heartland response that Blair was stirring up.

Clarissa came with us to the 1997 Waterloo Cup at Altcar. By now she had become a household name and was surrounded by hacks. With typical courage, she gave a number of interviews supporting coursing and field sports. Driving home after the third day, my wife Mary suddenly announced that she'd had a good idea.

'Oh, God,' Clarissa sighed, 'not another one.'

But, like all the best ideas, it was obvious as soon as she said it. Most of the problems in the countryside stem, in Mary's opinion, from the fact that the only television programme on the real countryside – the enormously popular *Out of Town* which ran for fifteen years – died with Jack Hargreaves in the early Seventies. This happened at a time when the countryside was becoming an irrelevance to the media and most of its attention was urban orientated. What was needed was a series of programmes showing the countryside as it really is. Wild with enthusiasm, we discussed the idea the whole way north and Clarissa suggested I jot down our ideas and send them to the production company who were making *Two Fat Ladies*.

'They would be mad not to take us up on it,' she said.

Insanity prevailed, they didn't take us up on the idea, and it was two years before divine intervention struck from quite another source. In 1999 Jane Root replaced Mark Thompson as Controller of BBC2. Jane had been co-owner of the production company, Wall to Wall, when I made my debut for them in Sophie Grigson's *Eat Your Greens*. She had also been Independent Commissioning Editor for BBC2 and thus our boss for *Two Fat Ladies*, so we go back a long way and I have the highest regard for her and her abilities. On inheriting BBC2, she pulled *One Man and His Dog* on the advice of Mark. Although this programme only had 700,000 viewers and was impossibly expensive to make, Jane received two million letters. This caused her to ask who was writing the letters, and she was told that they were from people who lived in the country. Further enquiries disclosed that nothing was being provided for these eleven million country-dwelling viewers and Jane sent Bob Long, of BBC Community Programming, to find a presenter who would be acceptable to the countryside.

Due to my presence at the marches and the rallies, my name came up and in March 1999 I received a call from Bob, whom I had never met, asking if he could come and see me at Jane's request. I receive a dozen approaches a week and was about to set forth to film the fourth series of *Two Fat Ladies*, but Jane's name was the key. So I met Bob at the airport and took him to Lennoxlove House in East Lothian (where I have the catering) for lunch. I think I assumed that it would be about alcoholism, but when Bob told me Jane wanted to commission a countryside programme you could have knocked me down with a feather.

I rushed to the kitchen and phoned Johnny who, luckily, was at home. I told him a possible miracle had happened and he was to stay where he was 'til I got there. Dear Johnny is used to humouring my enthusiasms, so he did. I dragged Bob from his coffee, threw him into my car and drove up to the Lammermuirs telling him *en route* of our previous idea. I explained to him that Johnny was the finest countryman I knew and that if he did not translate to camera then we must have him as a consultant. I also said that people in the countryside felt betrayed by the careless attitude the media has towards them, and the way they make their living.

'You are the channel,' I thundered, 'who made *Memories of an Irish RM* without a single fox-hunting sequence.'

Fortunately, we arrived at Johnny's at this point. Equally happily, Johnny was having one of his magic days when he could charm his way past the pearly gates and make calculus sound riveting (which I'm sure it is really), so he held Bob spellbound while he talked about hefting hill sheep for almost two hours. I drove Bob back to the airport and he promised to talk to Jane and come back with a camera to screen-test Johnny. At this time *Two Fat Ladies* was still very much an entity and, in any event, Jane would rightly not have given up a programme with so many million loyal viewers. I would gladly have ditched *Two Fat Ladies* for our new idea, but I couldn't, and I was at a loss to see how I would have the energy for both. Eventually, however, the programme was commissioned as a joint London – Scotland project and Bob Long became our Executive Producer.

I had a most agreeable lunch with Colin Cameron, Head of BBC Scotland, at Martin Wishart's in Leith. He recommended Esmé as Producer and Director. I met Esmé, by choice, in Valvonna and Crolla, the Italian delicatessen and restaurant in Edinburgh. Esmé is designer-Edinburgh, very chic and a vegetarian. Her only handle on the countryside was her friends, the Alexander brothers, who are keen point-to-pointers and supporters of the Fife Hunt. I was very straight and explained the importance of the programme to us personally. I also explained the danger of putting yourself in the front line, that I got regular death threats and that one had to be careful how one opened the post as spring pins, allegedly loaded with Aids-infected blood, were not uncommon. She said she would go away and think about it, and I was pleased when I heard she

I still have the bruise from Misty's kick

had agreed. I am a great admirer of Esmé, although she may be surprised to read this. She has enormous courage, both physical and mental, and a readiness to learn about and take on new challenges. I don't think she likes me much, but at least she has the generosity to admit when she's impressed.

I decided to have a rest after a most exhausting year. I booked ten days' holiday in Spain. Filming was due to start the week before Christmas, and Johnny and I had done our recce when, in early November, I went with some friends to southern Spain. On the third day of my sojourn I went off to bed and was suddenly gripped by the most awful pain. If you saw the movie *Alien 3* and remember the bit where the creature tears through her stomach, that's what I looked like. The six-year-old scar of my umbilical hernia had ripped out and the thing had strangulated. The villa I had rented was up a mountain and there was a thick fog that night. Eventually someone drove down to lead the ambulance up. The access to the villa was too steep for a stretcher so I had to walk: not a lot of fun. I was strapped into the ambulance. With hindsight I'm not quite sure why, as I had just walked to it, and we set off down the mountain only to take a wrong turn and get lost.

It took an hour and a half to reach the hospital and I felt every bump. I spent my time praying, telling God I had to go and fight for the countryside cause and couldn't die yet, and trying to ignore the fact that my great-uncle Kenneth had died of just such a hernia. I think I was the only person on the mountain that night who didn't think I might die, but frankly I didn't have time for dying. Johnny says he reckons that the cause has given many potential rural suicides the anger to go on. I think it saved me too, in my hospital in Fuengirola.

By 2.30 in the morning we reached the hospital. It took another three hours to get a surgical team and make a start, and then I was two-and-a-half hours in theatre and four days in intensive care. During the remaining ten days of my stay, Johnny rang every evening to give me moral support and progress reports. Neither of us mentioned the possibility that I couldn't go on – some things are simply *noblesse oblige*. I hobbled back to Scotland broken and in pain, weeping intermittently and curled up like a wounded animal to lick my wounds. Steve Sklair, who had been appointed Series Producer, came up for a day and we bonded for a couple of hours before Johnny arrived to discuss wildfowling. We were to begin filming that programme on 7 January 2000, with the hunting programme following two weeks later. Thank God I had the sense to veto that scheduling.

When Steve left, Johnny stayed on for a cup of tea and while we were talking about some peripheral subject I burst into tears. Poor Johnny, I don't think he'd ever seen me cry, even when he put his ferret down my neck. But still we never discussed postponement and I told no one that I'd been instructed to do nothing for six months. To paraphrase the Queen Mother, 'At last I felt I could look the countryside in the face.'

CHAPTER TWO

RUSHES HANGING WITH ICE

J At our meeting with the BBC on 13 October, we agreed that the programmes should cover as much of the British Isles as possible. There would be programmes in Scotland, Northern Ireland, Wales, the West Country, the Midlands, Northern England and East Anglia. Each programme would cover the link between field sports and conservation and how they were pertinent to each area.

East Anglia was chosen for the pilot, and the obvious choice of field sport was wildfowling, for which the county is historically renowned, with goose flighting being the most filmable. I knew that large numbers of pink-feet migrated to the Norfolk coast and grazed on sugar beet waste. Sugar beet is the principal crop in the area.

My contact in that part of the world was Richard Gledson, who had been factor to the Wemyss and Benson estates and was now with Lord Leicester at Holkham, whose land includes the salt marshes at Wells-next-the-Sea. As an initial approach, however, I decided to speak to William Heal, BASC's Director in East Anglia. The British Association for Shooting and Conservation was formed in 1981, when The Wildfowlers Association of Great Britain and Ireland expanded to encompass all shooting and conservation issues.

William was enormously helpful and encouraging about the project and suggested that I telephone Kevin Thatcher, the Chairman of The Wells Wildfowlers Club. I owe an enormous debt of gratitude to Kevin. He was the first person I asked to open the door into a very personal and sensitive world. Like all of us he was acutely aware that field sports have so often been misrepresented by the media, particularly over the last two decades. He listened with great courtesy as I explained our aims for the series. He quickly grasped the long-overdue need for a countryside programme that was representative and unbiased to those who live there. Before he could agree to allow the BBC to film, it was obviously necessary to gain the permission of his committee. Meanwhile, I contacted Richard and wrote to Lord Leicester, from whom I recieved a charming letter agreeing to allow filming at Holkham, as long as the wildfowlers were happy.

Early in November, Clarissa had a break in her incredible schedule which we used to go down and see the wildfowlers, stopping at Holkham to visit Richard and briefly to meet Lord Leicester. Kevin was away shooting on the Solway but we had the most entertaining dinner with the club's secretary and vice-chairman Russell Brumby and Mark Trett in Burnham Market or Chelsea-On-Sea, as it is known in the summer. Shortly afterwards Kevin telephoned with the news that his committee had agreed to our suggestions. It was a thrilling moment. We were off. Already my approaches to other areas of field sports were being received with great enthusiasm. Now all we had to do was persuade the BBC to appreciate just what they were being given.

Clarissa and I drove south on 6 January. Any journey with her, once you have got used to the driving, is always colossal fun and this was to be the start of 'The Great Adventure'. We seemed to laugh all the way to the windmill at Cley where we were to stay.

BBC directors love gimmicks and in an effort to impose one on this series, decided that the presenters should be seen to stay in increasingly unusual, if irrelevant, buildings, particularly those owned by the Landmark Trust. The pineapple building in Stirlingshire, for example, was deemed an absolute must despite the fact that it was miles from any filming location. The great windmill at Cley, which once milled all the grain from the surrounding polder, stands imposingly overlooking what was once one of the greatest ports in the British Isles. Now there are only reed beds through which the River Glaven meanders gently, but the windmill, in its most recent incarnation, was in fact a very comfortable place to stay. We thought of it affectionately some weeks later when we were staying in the Britannia House Hotel, Manchester's self-styled home of the ultimate dirty weekend.

When we arrived in Cley my spirits plummeted. Parked outside was an Argocat with a member of the team proudly displaying it to the rest of the crew. The sight of this vehicle brought back all my fears for the programme. At our discussions with Steve and Bob, neither of them appeared to be able to expunge from their minds the popularity of the motor-bike and

The great
windmill at Cley

Waiting for the
geese

sidecar in *Two Fat Ladies*. Despite my protestations that the vehicle to be used for the series must be compatible with those normally used in the countryside, they insisted that a viewer-attractive vehicle should feature in this programme. But to us, an Argocat is just as inappropriate in the wrong place – and this was the wrong place – as a Sherman tank.

That evening, Kevin, Mark, Russell and William Heal came to the windmill to meet the crew, and to show them a selection of magnificent wildfowling guns, including a monstrous percussion-cap 2 bore, the biggest shoulder gun I have ever seen. As we were talking, Russell caught sight of the Argocat through the window.

'What,' he said, 'is that thing doing outside?'

The explanation that this was to be the series vehicle was met with a stony silence. Finally, Kevin encapsulated all my anxieties.

'Wildfowlers do not use Argocats,' he said. 'You will be trivializing our sport if you suggest that we do.'

'The Argocat,' said Clarissa in a tone that invited no further discussion on the matter, 'will only appear where it should appear. And that won't be until we reach the Highlands.'

In 1863 Sir Ralph Payne-Gallwey, the great Victorian sportsman, wrote: 'The severe seasons of frost and snow and bitter wind that now and then occur in England, gladden the fowler's heart and he goes out in what is to him favourable weather. Whilst other men are sighing over unexercised hunters, or putting by their guns in rack or case 'til fields and woods are, from their point of view, fit places for sport, a fowler well knows that the more severe a frost may be, and the more biting the north and east winds, the better it is for him, for then are his fowl to be found and under such conditions will he do well to seek them.'

It was under just such conditions, when our breath condensed in clouds inside the house, and my mother wore an overcoat in bed and hunting stopped, that I remember the flurry of activity as my father packed to go north, goose flighting on the Tay. When I was a small boy he would sit me out of the way, on top of the chest of drawers in his dressing-room, and I would watch mesmerized as he assembled the oiled wool stockings, vests made of real string, jerseys, scarves and mittens, Balaclava helmet, corduroy breeches and the enormous grey hooded parka with an intriguing strap that buckled between his legs. Best of all, I remember the 8 bore, sent down from London by Holland and Holland, and the wet metallic clunk when the breech closed as the gun was assembled.

My father had the wonderful ability to create evocative pictures of the things he loved, and those which he wanted me to appreciate. Perched among the ivory hairbrushes and glass bottles of Truefitt and Hill's Oleaqua, an escapee from the nursery, I listened spellbound as he took me back through the centuries to a marsh filled with birdlife, where bitterns competed with the boom of distant surf. Deep in the rushes at the edge of a lagoon, a man with matted hair and clothes of skin waited patiently and hungrily for an unsuspecting pintail to swim within range. An explosion of energy, the frantic flailing stick, the squawk of alarm and the first of generations of wildfowlers trudged home, sodden and empty-handed.

A wisp of snipe flew overhead as men in rough-spun cloth harvested the marshes with net and decoy for the early manor houses. Hawks stooped and bows twanged. The first firearms roared and spluttered. Frost-covered reeds rattled in the wind as figures in sealskin hats and leather waders fumbled, with frozen fingers, for percussion caps as they struggled to make a living from the sale of birds to local markets. Bait diggers, stinking of the goose grease they used to protect themselves against the cold, fossicked for lugworms on the shore. This was nature at her most jealous and defiant: quicksands, spring tides, snow, rain, deadly mists and the spirits of the marshes who lured men to their deaths.

With the coming of the railways the birdsong was drowned by the sound of gunfire, as marshes and estuaries were commercially overshot to meet the demand for wildfowl in the expanding cities. Now these enchanting places are controlled by wildfowling clubs, and the most unique and challenging sport is carefully preserved.

At 5.45 am on Friday 7 January we met Kevin, Russell, Bob and Mark at the end of the Wells Beach Road. Mark had his skiff already in the water with the outboard running. Clarissa and I were ferried across the Wells Channel with Rod, the cameraman, perched in the bows, filming. We were deposited on East Hills, where we waited whilst Mark returned for the others. Apart

It's cold on the marshes

from the lack of moon, conditions were not promising: no wind, a clear starlit sky and what has become a feature of our changed weather patterns, a mild January. The sound of the outboard disappeared as Mark went to collect the second load. Standing with Clarissa in the darkness, something occurred to me.

Our researcher had muttered vaguely about a three-quarter-of-a-mile walk to our positions for the flight. Four weeks previously Clarissa had undergone major surgery in a Spanish hospital. She also had a plate in her foot from a childhood riding accident that made walking on uneven surfaces, particularly in gumboots, extremely painful. It was typical of her that she had made absolutely no reference to this and although the operation had been much publicized, it clearly had not been taken into account when the location was chosen.

When I look back now on how wretched and ill I felt, my heart swells with affection for Johnny. He was facing the unknown for the first time – and the personal fears that rear their ugly heads during one's debut as a television presenter – and yet it was his good spirits and unwavering encouragement that carried me, the hardened professional, through.

As we waited for the others, with the sound of the water lapping at the shore, I said to Clarissa, 'Look, are you going to be okay? This could be further than we think.'

'Perfectly,' she replied, in the tone of voice that brooks no further discussion.

The rest of the crew and the wildfowlers disembarked, and we set off in an extended line up the beach. Kevin, Mark and Bob ranged ahead along a path they knew well enough to follow blindfold. The crew trailed in their wake under the increasing burden of cameras, tripods and sound equipment. Bringing up the rear, with a stoicism that was to be reflected in later programmes, was Clarissa, silent and determined, resplendent in knee breeches, loden coat and rabbit-skin cap. In her right hand, a sturdy walking stick and in her left, to assist her over the shingle, sand, mud and whatever else lay ahead, a totally useless lantern with a beam that pointed downwards, normally used to illuminate faces for night filming.

The movement of thousands of geese stirring on their shore roosts, as dawn breaks over the North Sea on a winter's morning, is thrilling music to a wildfowler. For someone who has never heard it before, this eerie, distant, welling sound makes the hair prickle on the back of the neck. As the slither of light widened, the first geese started coming over the sandbanks: small skeins of almost black, reptilian-looking brents, flying in low wavering lines and speaking like foxhounds on a scent. Then with the dawn came the pink-feet, silhouetted against a lapis lazuli sky. Skein after skein of them poured inland to their grazings on the sugar beet fields. The sheer volume of sound, the ceaseless 'ang-ang-anging' and whoosh of wingbeats was quite breathtaking.

Beside me, deep in the crab grass of a tidal creek, Kevin crouched like a cat. Peering upwards, his face obscured with camouflage netting, he gauged the height of the geese that passed over us, estimating the range of a safe shot.

'Much too high. Weather all wrong,' he whispered. And then, 'Watch out; a big skein is coming straight for us. Look for a single bird flying below the rest and wait for my word.'

Five hundred yards along the creek were Clarissa, Mark, Steve, Dave the soundman, and Rod, with the big triangular box-shaped camera. Somewhere behind me was Robin with the smaller camera, which looks like an old-fashioned cine-camera. But I don't believe either Clarissa or I were aware of any of them.

Geese flying in to feed on sugar beet fields

The phase of the moon and its effect on the tides, wind direction, temperature and availability of inland grazing all influence the flight patterns and height of skeins. Much deliberation among other wildfowlers had determined our position on the marsh. Ideally we could have done with some rain to bring them down or, better still, some snow. Even then, the chances of being in the right place for a successful and sensible shot on that whole expanse of coastline were fairly remote, but that is one of the joys of goose flighting. In my case I was more than happy just to watch and hear one of nature's most enthralling spectacles.

By eight o'clock the marshes had become alive with birdsong and activity. Gulls shrieked, long-beaked red-legged oystercatchers flew by, pinging shrilly. Little shore larks tseeped. A trip of dunlin whisked past and redshanks, the sentinels of the marsh, set up a frenzied harsh piping as a hen harrier appeared briefly, saw us and slid away over the dunes. To complete this enchanting picture, a grey seal pup followed us along the creek as we walked down to join Clarissa and the crew. Steve summed up the morning succinctly and in the best White-City terminology: 'Bloody wonderful. Great telly.'

We trudged happily back to the boat and, eventually, to a well-earned breakfast at Nelson's in Wells. Over a hearty fry-up, the matter of a series vehicle was again raised. Our original suggestion, that a beaten-up old farm Land Rover would be very much more fitting for our journeys, was finally accepted. The question remained, one day into filming, of where to get one at short notice in strange territory. Mark, again illustrating the relationship the wildfowlers have

with the rest of the community, referred us to his mate Queenie, the manager of the amusement arcade. With a little persuasion Queenie loaned us his pride and joy: a C-registration, blue, truck-cab Land Rover with a white roof and an open back. This splendid vehicle, customized with the panache only a Land Rover fanatic can achieve, lacked but one thing to make it perfect: a step on the passenger side. This made things difficult for Clarissa. The days are gone when she could leap into the saddle with ease! It did, however, provide Steve with the opportunity to further his relationship with Clarissa. Whenever we had to get in and out of the Land Rover, something we were required to do several times a day, there would be stentorian cries of 'Buttock boy' from all sides, and there is photographic evidence of Steve, puce-faced, bending to the task. Queenie's subsequent refusal to sell us the vehicle led to terrible difficulties of which much more anon.

The wildfowlers had agreed to take us out again the following day. They were, however, deeply concerned about the effect that another long trudge in and out of the marshes would have on Clarissa. Paradoxically the only vehicle that could achieve this was the despised Argocat and so, after some discussion, it was decided to approach English Nature for permission to take the Argocat across the Wells Channel at low tide that afternoon, and along the foreshore in the morning. It is an indication of the excellent relationship that exists between the wildfowlers and English Nature that they readily agreed to allow this vehicle on the marshes.

In the stygian gloom of the following morning Kevin, Russell and I set off to approach our position for the morning flight from the lane that leads out to the mudflats. This was to illustrate the sort of journey wildfowlers would usually have taken across the salt marshes. With Robin

ABOVE: Mark Trett has a go
LEFT: I find a friend

gamely in tow with the smaller camera we set off into the pre-dawn darkness. Crossing oily planks over deep, sinister tidal creeks, past pools of brackish water with a cold sea breeze in our faces, we followed a path of incredible antiquity.

Men have hurried along here to catch the sunrise for centuries, carrying nets and traps and decoys, hawks, longbows, crossbows, snaphaunces, flintlocks and percussion-cap sporting guns. Now they bring heavy modern shotguns: 8 bores, 10 bores and 3-inch-chambered 12 bores, pitting themselves against the wiles and vagaries of nature. It was almost certainly the first time a BBC cameraman had been along it. We were following in the footsteps of the great writers, wildlife artists (and keen wildfowlers) and naturalists whose work has thrilled generations of enthusiasts: Col. Peter Hawker, Sir Ralph Payne-Gallwey, Denys Watkins-Pitchard, 'BB', JG Millais, Frank Southgate, Sir Peter Scott, Archibald Thorburn, Abel Chapman and William Booth; visiting Victorian gentlemen gunners and trophy hunters who came here in the days of the mania for taxidermy, and local pre-war goose guides, Pat Cringle, Gunner Howell, Sam Bone and the one-legged man known as 'The Mawkins'. Consumed with a sense of history I splashed enthusiastically and unnecessarily in and out of puddles for the benefit of future viewers, oblivious of the first rule of television: footage shot in the dark is of no interest.

We knew before we left, from the stars and the position of the tide, that the geese would come in far too high for a shot, but our brief was to engage Kevin and, in Clarissa's case, Mark in dialogue about wildfowling and the activities of their club. Hunkered down in the marsh grass, we listened as the wonderful cacophony of sound reverberated along the coastline with the rising dawn as 30,000 geese followed their flight paths to the sugar beet fields.

Kevin and I talked about his passion for the sport, his love of the marshes and how the phenomenon taking place above us was a classic example of field sports, conservation and farming working together successfully. This is the indivisible thread that is so misunderstood in our urban-dominated modern world. By the end of the Second World War, disturbance by a local ack-ack range had virtually driven the migrating pink-feet from their roosts. Those that remained were at risk from the right – available to everyone – to shoot or, more precisely, to carry arms on the foreshore. All too frequently, unprincipled pot-hunters dug themselves into the sand and shot geese as they returned to the roosts.

In 1952 concerned local wildfowlers formed themselves into a club to protect the remaining geese, and to preserve for posterity an ancient part of the history and heritage of the area. The population of pink-feet has risen annually through the club's efforts to protect them on their shore roosts, and through the co-operation of landowners, who welcome the geese feeding on the waste left behind by the sugar beet harvesters.

Membership of the club is restricted to 120 members who must live within a certain radius of the town. Bag limits are strictly controlled and aspiring members undergo a rigorous twelve-month probationary period, in the company of an experienced member, before election. They must prove to be proficient in gun safety, competent to shoot without wounding, able to identify quarry game from protected species, and have a thorough knowledge of the marshes and tides. Even wildfowlers who have known the marshes for years are capable of being marooned when the marshes are flooded by a flash tide, or stuck out there by a sudden sea mist. That is the time, when they are freezing cold and terrified, that the ghost of the woman who was lost searching for her fisherman husband can be heard calling for him, and their retriever tucks his tail between his legs and howls.

We discussed the pressures of urban spread, weekenders, the suburbanization of rural Britain and the threat from political interference to their sport. We talked about the role wildfowlers play in the area, and how club funds – raised from subscriptions, raffles, stalls and the auction of paintings by the artist members of the club – are used to benefit the community after club expenses have been met. This year they sponsored the local Under Tens' Football Club. In other years the money has gone to the local cottage hospital, and to the hospice.

We talked about the different backgrounds of the club members.

'As with the rest of field sports, we have members from all walks of life,' Kevin told me. 'Today, for example, you have an operating theatre technician, the manager of a caravan park, a retired gamekeeper and a 747 pilot. We have fishermen, farm labourers, a canon, doctors, the

Estuary mudflats at Blakeney Point

usual broad section of the community. One of the clubs up the coast even has a *Vogue* model. Leaving aside the BBC,' he said with a smile, 'our guests at the moment are a television celebrity and a hill farmer from Scotland. The Greener 8 bore you are using belongs to our Treasurer, a retired general manager of the Hong Kong and Shanghai Bank. The fascination of wildfowling and the magic of the marshes attract every sort of person and, subject to the election rules, anyone can be a member.'

As the last stragglers flew over us, we discussed the endless adjustments wildfowlers have to make to conform with changes in legislation and to co-operate with conservation and management groups. Many had already started to use non-toxic shot before lead shot was banned. Due to the excessive price of Bismuth and Tungsten matrix, as opposed to lead options which are nearly four times the price, many wildfowlers load their own cartridges. This hobby adds a further interest to the sport.

Kevin described the marshes and coast in the spring after the pinks have left for Iceland: the wild flowers, birdsong and rare summer and autumn visitors, such as the wood sandpipers, bitterns, bearded reedling and avocets, black-tailed godwits, little stints, spotted redshanks, blue throats and Montagu's harriers. His knowledge was encyclopaedic and it was fascinating listening to him. I suppose we must have talked almost non-stop for the best part of three quarters of an hour.

'Pretty well covered it,' I congratulated myself. On our way back across the saltings it occurred to me that the programme was only going to be half an hour long and there were still five days' filming ahead.

C   Our Lords and Masters of Government no longer encourage the teaching of English History in schools, no doubt to allow the children to become vassals of European or American states without noticing. You think I'm joking? My twenty-four-year-old god-daughter, at her fine grammar school in Birmingham, did 'Cattletrails of Abilene and Kansas' as her GCSE history project. There was no English option. Sadly this means that they miss out on a most exciting piece of British history in which a small group of friends, in a small part of Norfolk, changed the world in the mid-eighteenth century. I struggle to remember the Thirty Years' War or Marlborough's battles, but the names of Billy Coke, Turnip Townshend and Robert Walpole are as exciting to me now as they were when they started the Agricultural Revolution.

I began to talk enthusiastically about seed drilling, crop rotation and the 'new husbandry' when Steve had the strange idea of dressing Johnny, me and Lord Leicester (the present Coke of Norfolk) in eighteenth-century costume while we discussed such matters in front of Holkham Hall. Whilst I went weak at the knees at the thought of such well-turned calves in knee breeches – Johnny has great legs from louping up and down heather hills although I could only fantasize about Lord Leicester's legs – I couldn't see it as great viewing. Fortunately Steve was just fantasizing too!

Holkham Hall

When the Royalists had followed the future Charles II returned from exile, in 1660, they brought back new technical knowledge from Holland. Apart from the huge changes their knowledge brought to the shooting scene, they had discovered land drainage and they drained the Fens, those huge wetlands which had remained unchanged since Hereward the Wake held out against the Normans. With access to all this newly regained land, prosperity increased and with it the desire to improve the crops and animals that it supported. Billy Coke had inherited substantial estates at Holkham and was a man with a lively and enquiring mind. I love the story of how, observing a cabbage field infested with caterpillars which were destroying the crop, he turned 200 ducks loose in the field. They devoured the insects without harming the crop. Now there's organic for you.

William Coke was a man of great inventiveness. Apart from selective breeding to enlarge and improve his cattle and sheep, he designed himself a type of hard hat which became known as the Billycock hat and was the forerunner of the bowler. He designed the hat because he was sick of having his top-hat knocked from his head by low branches whilst riding round the park. (Incidentally the bowler gets its name from the firm of Thomas and William Bowler who supplied the rabbit skins to Lock & Co., the hatters, to make their squatter version of the Billycock.)

If you go to Holkham, and I hope you will, you will see the huge pavilion where the great Southdown rams that changed lowland sheep farming for ever were sold. Whilst we were filming, Lord Leicester's factor told us that they had sold the last of the sheep from Holkham that day because the market was so bad. I shed a tear for the reversal of the Agricultural Revolution that this Government seems so determined to achieve. Mr Blair would, I feel, turn the whole countryside into a theme park for ramblers, with farmers as its rangers. He would rather we imported unsafe food from the Far East. You think I'm joking about the food? Just ask yourself where all those chicken legs at £1.99 for six come from, then think of the standards of hygiene in South East Asia.

One of the great crops of East Anglia is sugar beet. If there are large quantities of people who don't know that milk comes from a cow, I wonder how many there are who don't realize the pound, or should I say kilo, of sugar on your table comes from a beetroot? All root crops contain a large quantity of natural sugar, but it is most easily extracted from sugar beet. This ugly turnip-like vegetable is native to Germany and Central Europe and sugar was first successfully extracted from it by Andreas Marggraf in 1747. It was, however, resourceful Napoleon Bonaparte who really souped up production.

Until the fifteenth century sugar had been virtually unknown and vastly expensive: the sugar cane being native to Africa. But the Venetians, always looking for ways to expand their trading interests, started growing it on the Isle of Cyprus and it became available to the rich. However, it was not until the sugar plantations of the West Indies began to flourish, in the seventeenth century, that sugar dropped in price. The triangular trade that shipped goods to Africa and slaves to the Caribbean brought back sugar, on its final leg, to Europe. Sugar is highly addictive and hundreds of Africans died in foreign cane fields just to supply the ever-increasing demand for sugar.

In order to keep his subjects in sugar, Napoleon perfected the art of extracting it from the beet and so was born an industry that virtually destroyed the sugar-cane industry. Today half the 174 million tons of sugar produced annually in this country comes from sugar beet, and the figure would be much higher were it not for Tate & Lyle's interest in Caribbean sugar-cane plantations. Britain has one of only three cane sugar refineries in Europe, the others being in France and Portugal. The Government sets quotas for sugar beet which are paid at a set rate. Last year Quota A, the highest priced, was set at 104 million tons and Quota B at 104,000 tons; everything else is Quota C and must be exported and sold for what the farmers can get, which is difficult, because large supplies of cheap beet come in from Central Europe and depress prices. The industry is in difficulties. The alternative is to replace the beet crops with winter wheat and only grow enough to supply the higher-priced quota.

This is not good news for the geese. Every day the pink-feet fly inland to feed on the harvested sugar beet crops. The geese do not eat the growing beet tops, they only like them after they have lain on the ground for a couple of days. The farmers harvest the crop and leave the tops for the geese to clean up. The geese devour these gratefully and leave behind a substantial gift of guano – goose shit to the less refined – to enrich the field.

At Holkham you hear the sound of geese feeding everywhere. Johnny and I went out with John King, Lord Leicester's Head Keeper. Mr King told us the facts you have just read while the geese fed, rose and settled before us. Johnny reminded us of the country maxim that sheep graze, goats tear and geese pluck, which explains why geese are not welcome on winter wheat: they can

We shan't be short of sugar

destroy a wheat field overnight. In the Scottish Islands farmers are paid a subsidy for the grass the geese destroy; however, it is unlikely that the Government will wish to subsidize the damaged crops of coastal East Anglia, which raises the question of what happens to the geese. Wild geese are not allowed, by law, to be sold onto the food market but surely, with the build-up of such large flocks of geese, there is scope for relaxing this rule somewhat. I can vouch for the fact that they are quite delicious to eat.

Now it would not be good television for Johnny and me to pontificate on sugar beet standing in the middle of a muddy field, so we devised a charming interlude wherein I persuade Johnny to humour me by pulling up enough sugar beet to refine into a 2 lb bag of sugar. After much joshing, and tasting the raw beet which was revolting, I climbed into a beet harvester and cropped

four tons to his measly fifteen hand-pulled beets, which weighed approximately 30 lbs! The harvester was a model of modern engineering. On a bitterly cold day the driver was wearing only dungarees and a light jacket as his cab is heated. It has a radio as well and the most enormous amount of equipment for setting the levels of the cropping blades, the depths of the digging tines and the weighing of the harvested crop. It is amazingly high-tech. I was brought up to drive everything, but I must admit that this is my largest vehicle to date. It was heady stuff. I had to drive the vast monster directly at Rod, the cameraman, stopping as close to camera as possible. Intrepid of him, I thought, especially after his efforts to kill me on the long trek across the salt marshes.

All that sugar beet made me think of John Fothergill, the legendary landlord of the Spread Eagle at Thame, whose favourite party trick was to serve dishes which looked quite other than they were and so surprise his customers. One of his great successes was bortsch made from sugar beet. As a white soup it would not be expected to taste of beetroot, but having tasted the beastly things, I doubt very much that it did.

When Johnny and I were researching last November we took a detour to look at Houghton, the seat of the Marquis of Cholmondeley, and the God who smiles on our programme took us round a certain way as we looked for a pub for some lunch. Through the fallow deer fencing we saw hundreds of milk-white deer. The white hart is a creature of legend, the vision of which turned tyrants into saints and sent debauched barons screaming from their wicked ways and

ABOVE: Deer-hound coursing
LEFT: Houghton Hall

packing for pilgrimages. Now, before the more pedantic among you point out that a hart is a four-year-old red deer stag, stop and ask yourselves how many white fallow stags you have seen?

The present Marquis's grandfather, exhibiting a gentle eccentricity, liked everything white. He had white doves, white dogs and white deer in the park. It was this fallow herd, we subsequently discovered, that provided the breeding stock for the ones we had just stumbled across. In order to show that the sugar beet residue, once the sugar is removed, is turned into pellets for animal food, it was necessary to be seen feeding it to some beast or other and Johnny wouldn't really do – although I conned him into munching some on camera by pretending to taste it and declaring it yummy. (He fell for it every time, but don't try it, it's filthy!) So our white fallow deer fitted the bill perfectly and David Cholmondeley kindly allowed us to film at Houghton.

The deer are actually part of a breeding stud run by an American called Todd Bruno. It is a very sophisticated affair with electronic breeding programmes and specially built veterinary sheds. White deer from Houghton are sold to parks all over the world. We went and fed beet pellets to Boris, a six-year-old white stag with a penchant for posing majestically on any raised bit of ground. It is this characteristic part of their natural mating ritual which renders the breed so popular as park animals, and very fine he looked.

Only the finest specimens are sold on; the rest are sent off to be slaughtered for venison. Roe and red deer are the breeds most usually found on a menu, but Todd says they are establishing a rise in the popularity of the fallow deer. I had imagined that the skins would be a premium product – as unbleached doeskin – but apparently the skins are too small for the furniture market, which is the main modern-day buyer. Oh, how one pines for the feel of buckskin breeches – interpret that as you as you choose, dear reader!

We had another treat in store that Saturday. The Deer-hound Coursing Club were meeting at a local farm. Bernard Hendy, their Chairman, had readily agreed to my request to allow the BBC to film. It was a wonderful opportunity for the crew to witness coursing, possibly the most misunderstood of all field sports. Lord Watson, at the introduction of his shambolic Protection of Wild Mammals (Scotland) Bill before the Rural Affairs Committee, described coursing as an activity in which a baying mob takes pleasure in the chase and savage killing of a mammal, purely in the name of sport. Nothing could be further from the truth.

Deer-hounds are a breed of great antiquity. Descendants of the Alaunts – big gaze-hounds used on all types of large game that were brought to Scotland and Ireland when the Celts moved across from Europe. Originally deer-hounds were used to hunt red deer on the old tainchel system, similar to the Saxon hayes, where game was driven into narrowing defiles, either man-made or natural. Hunters, plagued no doubt by midges, waited with spears, bows and hunting knives. Later on hunting methods changed with the Normans and, although the tainchel system continued well into the eighteenth century, deer-hounds were more commonly used to course deer. Deer were stalked with two or three deer-hounds, until they were close enough to be slipped. The deer-hounds would overhaul a beast, knock it off course with a hard blow to the shoulder, and then kill it with a clean bite to the neck before it had a chance to recover.

As the rifle developed and became more high-powered and accurate the deer-hound was made increasingly redundant. Some stalkers kept them to track a beast wounded on the hill, but inevitably the bloodlines became mongrelized until only a few pure-breds were left. Archibald McNeil of Colonsay kept the breed going in the nineteenth century, and we must be grateful to Marjorie Bell, Norah Hartley and Anastasia Noble, with her famous Ardkinglass Kennels, for preserving the breed intact until the present day.

As a result of an increase in gangs poaching deer with dogs, often lamping them at night, an Act was passed, in the early Fifties, banning the hunting of deer with dogs in Scotland. In an effort to keep the hunting instinct alive in deer-hounds, Kenneth Cassels, author of the definitive book on deer-hounds, *A Most Perfect Creature of Heaven*, held the first deer-hound meeting in 1954 on Dava Moor, coursing blue hares under National Coursing Club (NCC) rules. There are now around seventy enthusiastic members who attend meetings up and down the country.

Unusually, many deer-hounds seen at coursing meetings also appear in the show ring, including Crufts, and unlike most show dogs they have remained little changed from their medieval ancestors. They stand thirty inches at the shoulder and weigh about 100 lbs. Most deer-hound coursing meetings are walked up; this one, however, was driven and we arrived just as John King, Lord Leicester's Head Keeper, resplendent in the Holkham livery of Billycock hat and tweed shooting suit, was bringing the beat in. There was a moment of great hilarity when poor Steve, in giving instructions to the crew, found himself in the wrong place at the wrong time and was subjected to a harangue from all sides.

'Hare coming through. Don't move. Come this way. Stand still. Quick, for God's sake!'

He stood absolutely rigid as a hare popped through the hedge and sat down beside him. The moment was improved on seconds later when an inquisitive deer-hound gave Clarissa a goose supreme. The sharp end of nearly one-hundred-weight of deer-hound between the buttocks produced a yell of appreciation that must have been heard in the next county.

With order restored and a new beat under way we were able to observe these magnificent animals in action. There were a number of obvious differences from the coursing we were accustomed to. For one thing the flinty ground of a recently harvested sugar beet field would have wrecked any greyhound, but then their initial turn of speed far outstrips any deer-hound's. For that reason the NCC stipulation of a minimum law of eighty yards for a greyhound, the distance a hare is given before the greyhounds are slipped, is reduced to at least fifty yards. A hare's speed is so great, relative to a deer-hound's, that they can easily disappear from view and, like all gaze-hounds, a deer-hound packs up as soon as it loses sight of the hare. We saw quite a number of young dogs gallumphing back to their owners with hopeful silly grins, having become unsighted.

Like the rest of coursing under NCC rules it is a judged competition of speed, stamina and agility. The aim, contrary to propaganda, is not to kill hares and only those that are fit and healthy are coursed. It was a super afternoon in the company of delightful and open-hearted people who had responded to the intrusion into their day with great good humour. I was intrigued to know what the crew thought of it and found to my delight that they were universally fascinated by the majesty and obvious enjoyment of the deer-hounds, and the fact that the hares were in no way distressed by being coursed.

You will have unerringly followed the skein unravelling in this chapter, from the geese that flew over the marshes and ate the tops of the sugar beet in the sugar beet fields, to the sugar beet pellets that the white deer fed on, to the deer-hounds that once hunted them. The last local interest brought us back to the marshes, and to bait digging. We were taken out onto the sands in the much-discussed Argocat. Johnny and I meandered across the sands, Johnny with

The goose dinner

his scarf wrapped fetchingly over his flat cap as he was unable to bring warmth to his ears by the power of positive thought alone. I spied the bait digger and cried happily, 'Look, a man.' I can usually manage enthusiasm over that line. Kevin has been a bait digger on the sands for thirty-five years. He digs lugworms to sell as fishing bait to order. He needed 55,000 for a customer that morning. Lugworms are the marine equivalent of earthworms: they live on the nutrients in the sand. It struck me that in this modern mechanized world of altered values, the sheer hard physical labour, isolation and indeed danger of this job would have the bureaucrats throwing up their hands in horror, yet I have seldom met a man so at peace with his surroundings or so content in himself.

The supply of bait is a large industry within the fishing community. In the Norfolk Broads they have slot-machines which supply a packet of live maggots for 50 pence, but there was something surreal about Kevin's lonely chore of collecting a huge number of worms. We left him as the tides began to run and drove back to the car park in the Argocat. I have to admit it was useful for such things. Useful, that is, until it got stuck in the boggy sand. Everyone piled out to shift it, telling me firmly to stay put. I was sitting there in splendid isolation, as I thought, until I looked over my shoulder and saw that Dave had not moved either, but was sitting with his sound baton held firmly erect.

'Soundmen,' as Johnny said later, 'obviously don't push.'

In the car park I nearly met my death. I was sitting in the Land Rover talking to Johnny, when a member of the crew decided to fool around and drove the Argo to the top of an adjacent shingle bank. Not surprisingly, the thing stalled at the highest point – he panicked and tried to pull on the handbrake, failed, and half a ton of machine careered down the bank towards the Land Rover. I actually thought my last hour had come and remembered clearly that my will still contained an instruction that I was to be buried in a burning Viking galley (this had seemed like a good idea in my drinking days, and I had never got round to changing it). Johnny, gallant friend that he is, didn't leap out but flung an arm round me and pulled me to his manly chest which simply meant that we would go together. He was always the hero and I the pragmatist! God, however, was still with us, for at the last moment the great machine slid on the shingle and bounced off the wheel.

To try to kill a favoured presenter once, by making her walk miles in the pitch dark over uncertain marshy ground for the wildfowling programme, within weeks of a life-threatening operation, is careless. Twice is unacceptable. That particular member of the team wasn't with us for programme two – he was, in any event, a man who had lived in the country rather than a countryman!

The BBC were still unable to sever the umbilical cord linking me to my cooking prowess on *Two Fat Ladies*. Whilst we were all agreed that it was necessary to be seen to consume the fruits of our hunting and gathering, where applicable, I had to utilize the steeliest gaze in my repertoire to whip them off the line that I should always do the cooking.

The goose dinner filmed at the Three Horseshoes at Wareham was a memorable party. We and the wildfowlers dined on the most delicious pink-foot, cooked to perfection by Ian, the co-owner of this excellent pub. It was a perfect opportunity for the nation to witness Johnny's legendary carving skills, even though he was travelling, on this occasion, without his favourite ivory-handled knives. Despite the fact that it was being filmed, the evening quickly developed into the best sort of sporting dinner party.

J No one who was there will ever forget the landlord and Clarissa's joint rendition of 'There'll always be an England' on the Pianola, and Robin rose yet further in our estimation by his virtuoso performance of 'Come to the Cookhouse Door' on Bob Appleby's circular hunting horn.

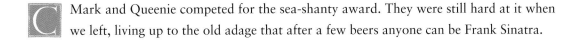

C Mark and Queenie competed for the sea-shanty award. They were still hard at it when we left, living up to the old adage that after a few beers anyone can be Frank Sinatra.

CHAPTER THREE

SEA MISTS
AND FAIRY
CATTLE

J We came to Mull for a variety of reasons, one of the most important being that three of the central components for the programme were all there – stalking, fish farming and creel fishing – within reasonable driving distance. Another great advantage was that I knew the island well from numerous happy family holidays, and I had friends with stalking who were prepared to help. The stag season starts on 1 July and finishes on 20 October. Hind stalking runs from 21 October to 15 February and is the period when old hinds, and ones that are barren, as opposed to yeld, are culled in order to maintain a healthy herd and to relieve suffering amongst the old and ill. Ideally this is done as early in the season as possible.

We had a meeting with Esmé, the Producer and Director, and Chloë, the Assistant Producer – both of whom appeared to be young enough to be my daughters – at BBC Queen Street in Edinburgh on the Tuesday after our return from Norfolk. We discussed the Mull programme, and the later one on fox-hunting. Unlike Norfolk which was, after all, intended as a pilot shoot, these programmes were discussed in enormous detail and copious notes were taken. I found this process tremendously encouraging.

Esmé has the professionalism to listen with great courtesy and patience, a quality that, considering the sensitivity both of the subjects and the people who were prepared to be involved, went a considerable way to relieving some of the anxieties I had about the programmes.

There were subsequent meetings after Esmé and Chloë had been to Mull, visited the contributors and prepared their research. The Highlands offered us tremendous scope: distilleries, tweed production, fish farming, prawn fishing, skiing and, of course, field sports. Field sports alone generate £40 million annually to the Scottish economy, a figure that Scotland can ill afford to lose, and a fact that Lord Watson appears to have overlooked in his eagerness to bring forward, as a priority for the new Scottish Parliament, a Bill to ban hunting with dogs.

Shooting, fishing and particularly stalking have been portrayed as a rich man's indulgence. We wanted to show the other side of stalking: the work that goes into deer forest management, and how the maintenance of a healthy controllable deer population is dependent, in part, on the hind cull. Red deer are woodland creatures and given the chance, as the Forestry Commission knows only too well, still would be. The destruction of the great Scottish forests of Jed, Ettrick and Caledonia – which were whittled away over the centuries as the population expanded – accelerated during the Industrial Revolution and the expansion of agricultural improvements. This drove the homeless deer to seek new habitats in the open hill ranges of the Highlands. Much the same thing happened to the red deer in England: most of the population now lives on Exmoor and Dartmoor. As a forest beast, red deer lived singly or in small groups depending upon the season. With the destruction of their cover, red deer find safety and security by herding together, although stags and hinds live separately except during the rut.

It is this imposed behavioural pattern, and the landscape in which they now live, that makes the stalking of red deer a unique feature of Scotland. In 1750 the red deer population was described as 'substantial'. Stalking as we now know it was a thing of the future, and deer taken for the larder were either coursed or hunted in the old tainchel system where beaters drove a whole herd into some convenient place of entrapment, such as the narrow end of a glen or a bog. During the last fifty years of the eighteenth century, the expansion of the golden hoof into the Highlands – as sheep graziers offered huge rents for grazings – led to a dramatic decline in deer numbers. By 1810 only half a dozen of the now recognized 450-odd deer forests held any quantity of deer.

In the 1850s, the wool price collapsed, sheep numbers dropped and the deer started to return. Improvements in rifle-making and Queen Victoria's passion for Scotland led to the development of deer forests as prime land use on many Highland estates, and the area covered by recognized deer forests rose, by the end of the nineteenth century, to two million hectares. To date, this figure is now at over three million hectares, or 37% of Scotland's land mass, supporting a red deer population of some 350,000.

There are thousands of part-time jobs supported by stalking, with 500 or so professional stalkers. The sale of venison from both farmed and wild deer comes to about £10 million, a figure that fluctuates depending upon the imports from New Zealand. There is a fairly brisk trade in 'stalkers' perks': eye-teeth, prized by the Germans for some reason – your dressy German sports a set of eye-teeth cufflinks. Eye-teeth were once so popular that a stalker with a bag of them could have a good time in the Reeperbahn without reaching for his wallet. Pizzles and scrotums can fetch as much as a tenner for a particularly fine set, and are sold as taste sensations in the better sort of Far Eastern restaurant. A stag's scrotum actually makes a very fine tobacco pouch, an opportunity the smoking accessory trade appears to have overlooked. Sinews, taken off the forelegs complete with dew claws, go to the Chinese food market. Antlers have a variety of uses: in this country they become knife handles or buttons, etc. In Bangkok they are converted into aphrodisiacs.

The approach to Mull from Oban is hugely picturesque: the islands of Kerrera and Lismore; the seagulls and the sea; Duart Castle which glares proud and defiantly at Argyllshire; Craignure Bay and the pier. The intention was to film Clarissa and me on deck, chatting in a general and enthusiastic way about Mull and hind stalking on the way over. This conversation would, no doubt, have been absolutely fascinating on its own, but to entertain those whose interest may not have been entirely focused on deer forest management, and to conform with the BBC's desire for humorous interludes, I had the idea that Clarissa should shoot sweets at the seagulls with a

The SS Isle of Mull

Feeding the seagulls

catapult. We used to do this on every crossing to amuse the children, and it is in fact great fun watching the gulls trying to catch the sweets in mid-air. This appealed to Esmé's sense of humour, so we drove back into Oban and bought a catapult from the fishing shop at the top of the town, and an enormous bag of football-shaped chocolate sweets from Woolworths.

Sadly, by the time we were ready to leave, the mist had come down and we had to film the catapult sequence in a variety of different locations to stop the lenses getting wet. The *Isle of Mull* ploughed through thick banks of moisture-laden mist and at one point, when the mist lifted for a moment, I seized the opportunity and pointed at the Morvern Peninsula.

'Look Clarrie – Mull,' I said.

'Where?' she said, as the curtain of mist came down again.

Finally, damp and dejected, we packed it in and retreated to the bar. To distract us Chloë produced two vast wedges of close-typed paper. In quite staggering detail the whole island had been researched, practically down to the last acre and, particularly for our programme, stalking, salmon farming, creel fishing and cheese-making each had a separate section. There were programme outlines and a synopsis and, finally, the filming schedule. Every moment of every filming day was catalogued with infinite care. According to this document, the week's filming was going to run like clockwork. It was a triumph of energy and effort: how they managed to produce it in such a short space of time was beyond me. To keep the drips running off her loden coat from wetting her bottom, Clarissa sat on her copy.

The one thing that hadn't been taken into account was the weather. As I know only too well, Mull has its own mini-climate which consists mainly of rain. February is marginally wetter than the rest of the year, and for the filming it had really pulled out the stops. Front after front rolled in from the south-west bringing deluges of rain, or mist which totally obscured the landscape. The week had been carefully split in two, based at the Gruline Home Farm in the centre of the island for the first few days, whilst we filmed hind stalking and fish farming, moving to Glengorme Castle for creel fishing and cheese-making. The beautifully prepared schedule was knocked sideways by the weather on the first day. Thick mist cancelled the hind stalking. Rough seas made filming salmon farming and creel fishing out of the question. We hurried north to the cheese farm. It, at least, could be filmed inside. We arrived as the mist lifted and the sun shone with winter brilliance. It became a feature of that extraordinary week, shuttling backwards and forwards across the island, grabbing bits and pieces of filming wherever we could. Because we hadn't been able to persuade Queenie to sell us his Land Rover, we had acquired, for filming continuity purposes, and with enormous difficulty, a Land Rover similar to his. This vehicle was to prove a thorn in our sides until it was finally abandoned. On Mull, wherever we filmed, a large pool of oil was left behind as a memento of our presence.

We filmed a picnic scene and the Mull Little Railway in the pouring rain, with Chloë and Steve holding umbrellas over Robin and Shu and their cameras. When all else failed, we filmed linkage shots: an endless succession of driving scenes over which dialogue could later be dubbed. Sometimes actual conversations were taped with Robin and Dave, the soundman, crouching

Mull Little Railway

wetly in the back of the Land Rover whilst Clarissa and I steamed happily within, prattling inanely. We were always sodden, me especially. When we had driven triumphantly off the ferry, the open-backed Land Rover was overflowing with our kit. There were suitcases, rods and sticks, etc., and because so much of our filming was by now completely out of sequence, all this equipment had to be brought along every day, just in case we needed to fill in time, and film leaving the boat, or driving back on again when we left, or moving from Gruline to Glengorme. As a result all my bags and their contents – Clarissa's somehow were never included in this – were always sopping wet. At night my hotel room steamed and reeked as I tried to dry my clothes. In the morning I would religiously pack them all up again and load up the Land Rover. The crew were far too nice to mention that this was a ludicrous thing to do. On the last day Dave observed that if it had been him he would have filled the suitcases with newspaper.

It was a nightmare for the production team. Esmé smiled brilliantly and patiently as I bombarded her with streams of inconsequential and impractical suggestions, all of which I was sure would be of enormous help. Chloë smiled brilliantly and provided a constant supply of hot drinks and sandwiches. 'Buttock boy' Steve, who had now become 'Umbrella man', assured everyone that 'It'll be fine. It'll be okay. It can't go on forever like this for Christ's sake.' Robin and Shu fretted about their cameras and Dave became inscrutable.

Gradually, against all the odds, the programme began to take shape. The sea was calm enough one afternoon to film creel fishing, and the following morning we grabbed salmon farming. We filmed dog fishing – fishing for dogfish – at night, off the pier at Craignure, something I have spent so many happy hours doing with the children when we have stayed at Dalriada. We filmed zeroing the rifle with Lachie, the stalker, and we filmed Clarissa fishing from an Argocat borrowed from Lachie.

What continued to elude us, the focal point of the programme, was the stalk. As the week progressed, Esmé's smile became, just fractionally, tight round the edges. At night there were long telephone conversations to Lachie and the Meteorological Office. The logistics of staying on, or leaving and returning later, were discussed and dismissed as impossible. The season ended on 15 February, besides which some of the crew were already booked elsewhere. Filming the Waterloo Cup was due to start in little over a week and Clarissa and I had an enormous amount of work to do on the synopsis. Constructing the scene was out of the question. The weather simply had to improve.

Early on the last morning Lachie rang up to say that in his experience, and contrary to the Meteorological Office forecast, the next front of bad weather would not be due until late afternoon. He was game, if we got down there sharpish. Anything was worth a try and Esmé, Robin, Dave and I were with him by 9 am. Lachie had the estate Argocat chugging as we arrived and we were loaded and away by 9.15 am.

By ten o'clock we were unloading the gear fifty yards in front of the edge of a forestry plantation, with the hill stretching away through the gaps in the trees. The first move was to make our way down a steep glen, over a boulder-strewn burn and up the other side, where Lachie and I lay down for a spy. A group of perhaps thirty hinds, and some calves, were lying down or grazing peacefully in the shelter of a fold on a steep face about five hundred yards away. Behind me I could hear the crew getting their breath and readjusting their gear.

I think it was an extraordinary experience for us all, that day of filming on the hill, with Ben More towering in the distance and the occasional glimpse of Loch Scridain. If Lachie and I had

Fairy cattle

been on our own it would have been a fascinating and magical day for me in the company of a professional who knows his deer, and his forest, like the back of his hand. As it was, there was an air of desperation over the proceedings that increased as the day wore on. We prayed that the weather would hold. Lachie's forecast had been right in some respects and wrong in others. A front of sorts was beginning to come in but, with a drop in temperature, it was arriving in the form of snow showers and not rain. As long as it stayed like that we could continue to film.

Lachie was trying to work out how best to approach the hinds when another herd appeared over the skyline, moving ahead of the weather and above us. One old matriarch spotted us – they're always on the lookout for danger – or maybe it was a raven rising out of the forestry that gave us away. But from a stalking point of view, the fun was now on. I do not believe the crew had the remotest idea what lay ahead of us. Both groups of hinds were now alerted and, in an unhurried fashion, were moving slowly before the weather, in unison. We had been seen and the hinds were reassured that we were too far away to be a danger. It's when they scent but can't see you that they really get spooked. In due course they settled and started to graze again.

'They'll keep moving with the weather, looking for shelter,' Lachie told us. 'We must get ahead of them.'

We set off up the burn as quickly as we could, sharing the equipment between us: tripod, heavy camera, haversack, Dave's sound box and boom.

We slipped and slithered along the mossy bank, crossing and re-crossing the burn. Every so often Lachie would crawl up for a spy. When he came down the message was always the same: 'We must keep going.' At midday we called a halt and Lachie went for another spy. The snow squalls were falling more frequently now. When he came back he said, 'Now look, the wind is all wrong. To get in position for a shot we need to go another three miles.'

There would be nothing unusual about this on an ordinary day's stalking but, for the crew, it was something of a facer. It was a moving moment. Robin and Dave were clearly done in. Robin had rarely relinquished the camera, and on the occasions when I had carried it, I discovered how heavy and awkward it was, even for short distances. Dave, who had always given the impression that he worked strictly to some curious form of union rule which almost certainly would not include scrambling about a Highland deer forest in the wet, had done far more than I expected him to. He had complained for some days of a bad back, and he looked grey and pinched, but going on meant the chance of turning Esmé's first programme into a success, packing up meant failure. It had been a simply hellish week for her and although the stress must have been enormous she had never shown it.

'A doddle,' said Robin, hoisting up the camera. 'You okay, Dave?'

There was a slight pause before he replied, 'Absolutely perfect, ready when you are.'

'I think,' said Esmé, 'we should have a cup of coffee and something to eat first.'

We never discovered how far any of them could have gone on, because half an hour after we moved off a particularly violent snowstorm swirled across the hill. When it had passed, Lachie crawled round the side of a steep rocky shoulder for another spy. After a minute or so he beckoned me up beside him. Sheltering among the boulders in a broad corrie, about 100 yards away, were the hinds. We crawled back and loaded the rifle. Robin set up the camera and Dave assembled the sound gear. With Robin beside us and Dave a little way behind, we wormed our way up again. The hinds were beginning to graze now.

'See the one just to the left of that big boulder?' asked Lachie. 'She's seven years old and won't last 'til the spring.'

I could see her clearly through the scope, distinguishable from the others by her darker coat.

The hind turned broadside. I settled the rifle, thumbed over the safety, centred the recticle

End of a day's stalking

behind the shoulder and pressed the trigger. The .276 boomed and I heard Lachie say quietly, 'Hit.' When I looked through the scope the hind was down. We walked across to check that she was dead and I was relieved that it had been a clean kill. Gralloching was our next little job. Steve was keen to film this since it is always carried out immediately after a deer has been shot. Gralloching achieves three things: swift removal of the intestines ensures that the carcass does not become tainted and it considerably lightens the weight of a beast for the long drag back off the hill. It also reduces the risk of the flesh becoming bruised, diminishing its saleable value.

I held the hind by the legs whilst Lachie made his incision at the brisket, slit the skin down to the crotch, rolled up his sleeves and plunged his arms into the belly. Out of the corner of my eye I could see Esmé, white-faced and determined, directing Robin on the camera. Gralloching a deer is a fairly awesome sight if you have never seen it before, and Esmé was not only cold and exhausted, but she also does not eat meat. Her stoicism went beyond the call of duty and I could have hugged her. Unfortunately, BBC protocol forbids such familiarity between directors and presenters.

Clarissa's parting words to me had been 'Don't forget, if you shoot a hind I want the humbles.'

'Clarissa wants the humbles,' I told Lachie, as he heaved the stomach onto the ground. He gave me a long look.

'And what might the humbles be?'

'I'm not sure. The guts I think.'

'Well,' he said, wiping his knife on the ground, 'if Clarissa wants the humbles she can come and get them herself.'

With gralloching over the mood of the crew brightened considerably. We set off, Lachie and I dragging the hind by the legs. When we reached an area of hill accessible to the Argocat we left the hind to be collected later that day. I told Robin to pass me the heavy DV camera. Earlier in the day, as the crew struggled to keep up with us while we were trying to get ahead of the hinds, I had promised myself that I would carry the camera back off the hill. Tired, but happy, we eventually arrived back at the lodge. Against all the odds the week's filming had been successful: an old hind had been saved from a lingering death and food for the hoodie crows.

Deer forest management is, allowing for the difficulties of the landscape, much the same as any form of stock husbandry, but it is, perhaps, closest to extensive hill farming. A stalker will know the deer on his forest in much the same way as a shepherd knows his sheep. The health of deer is determined by stocking numbers relative to available grazing. One of the stalker's jobs is to see that this delicate balance is achieved by controlling numbers. Selectively culling runts, poor doers and those with genetic faults improves the size and carcass quality of the herd. The old, the weak and the ill are protected from a painful lingering death. A stalker with his rifle provides the same service that an abattoir does – probably more humanely. And at least while deer cannot be gathered in and loaded on to lorries – the terrain, and their temperament, makes this impossible – they have the dignity of dying on their own ground.

We had devised a story-line to preserve me from the impossible physical exertions of the stalk. It would have been an effort for me with my bulk at any time, and it was only two months since my operation. Besides the deer would, no doubt, have mistaken me in my loden jacket for a green hill far away! So, protesting for camera that Johnny had lied to me about the exertions involved, I took myself off fishing and had great fun nearly capsizing the Argocat on the river-bank. Then, tiring of my lack of success, I took myself off to an isolated telephone kiosk and rang the local salmon farm.

There was a time when salmon was a luxury. I can remember the excitement when the great fish would arrive through the post – overnight from the Scottish Highlands – laid on ferns and wrapped in a carrying bag constructed of woven rushes. It was always sent down to London in the guard's van of the sleeper. The fish would arrive within twenty-four hours of being caught and was lovingly cooked, either poached in a fish kettle or more occasionally in the oven, and served with the pomp that a special treat merits. My father had a friend who always served the salmon he had caught surrounded rather sombrely by laurel leaves. He said that only a laurel wreath was fit for the champion of fish. However, stocks of wild salmon are running low, the great fishing rivers are failing the rods who paid so highly for the privilege of a beat, and farmed

Left me waders at home

salmon has become a very obvious option. There is nothing new about farming the seas or raising domesticated fish. The Romans grew oysters on ropes and, we are told, raised red mullet in netted areas. Every great house and monastery of the Middle Ages had its stews or ponds for carp and perch.

In the 1960s enterprising owners of sea lochs began raising fish in caged areas inside the lochs. The fish were fed on what is known as 'industrial fish', basically krill, sand eels and the like, with enough shrimp to ensure the correct coloration. It is always easy to tell wild from farmed fish: the confined space in which farmed fish are reared prevents the salmon from exercising its tail muscles. If you pick one up by the tail you cannot grasp it firmly. In the early days of farmed fish, fishmongers used to lie about a fish's origins, but it is usually only necessary to ask to handle the salmon for them to go off to change the preferred denizen. Today almost every sea loch you pass has salmon cages in it. They are strange-looking Heath Robinson contraptions which give no hint of the complex constructions you will find if you visit one.

When we were filming on Mull the weather was dreadful, so it was with some trepidation that I set foot on the converted landing craft to travel into the waters of the loch. The fish farms are placed in the inner waters of the loch so that rough seas will not damage them, and they can be worked in all weathers, but therein lie some of the problems the industry experiences. The cages, and the loch floor, are not scoured of refuse and spilt food by the winter storms, precisely because they are in calmer waters. Tests in Loch Ailert have shown that although the loch flushes out in an eight-week cycle, the deeper areas are stagnant with waste and there is a reduction in the oxygen levels necessary for sustaining marine life. Moves are afoot to position the cages further out into the lochs, but firms are reluctant to incur the extra expense in lost man-hours and sea damage. Ulva Fish Farm is one of the best, and its cages are well out into the loch. Reay Whyte, the Manager, told me that during the recent storms he had felt seasick in his office, a Portacabin raised on a floating platform.

There is something truly surreal about a fish farm. It is basically a series of floating metal (Meccano-like) walkways dividing seemingly empty areas of water. There is no sound but the

Ulva Fish Farm

lapping of the waves and the gulls, until every so often, with a startling crack, a fish jumps. When you lean over the netted areas you can see swirls of movement like some science fiction movie where great monsters lurk. They are, of course, the salmon, and when they were fed on the pellets – which are monitored through huge tubes from a machine worthy of Captain Nemo – they thrashed and leapt and writhed like a single silver creature.

Ulva Fish Farm is owned by the huge Norwegian consortium, Hydroseafoods, who own 35% of the market share in Scotland, and also farm in Denmark, the Faroe Islands, Chile and Australia. Their losses, caused by salmon anaemia, are forcing them to sell to Marine Harvest, which is owned by Nutrio, another multinational with 25% of the Scottish salmon-farming market. If I feel uneasy that 60% of all salmon farming in Scotland is owned by one Dutch company, how do you think the Highlanders and Islanders feel?

The fish in the cages I visited were being harvested at between 12 and 14 lbs and that day they had taken 12,000 fish. Each fish is killed by being knocked on the head with a white plastic rod. This costs many man-hours, but it is the only way to ensure the fish is dead and avoid the internal bleeding caused by suffocation. It also prevents any scraping of the scales, caused by dying struggles, which might spoil the look of the fish for the fishmonger, although I imagine, at this size, most of them were destined to be cut into salmon steaks and fillets, or made into fish cakes. Smaller fish, of 4–5 lbs, are sold whole with a luxury label. There is now – horrors! – talk of a genetically modified salmon which will grow up to twelve feet long but, with any luck, the reality will never materialize.

In 1998 the British Isles reared 115,000 tons of salmon, rising to 120,000 in 1999. Very little is exported – only about 30 tons, mostly to France – which I surmise is mainly smoked. Norway, the other main exporter of farmed salmon raised 39,500 tons in 1999 of which 27,400 tons were exported. For us it is an industry that is revolutionizing the Highland economy provided, as ever, we can find the markets.

The two major problems that have hit the fish-farming industry are sea-lice and salmon anaemia. With wild salmon, the sea-lice die as they enter fresh water to spawn and so there is a natural monitoring. But with farmed salmon, there is no such natural process and so the lice infest the salmon's skin, causing loss of condition, poor health and even death. The treatment with chemicals, mostly the organophosphate dichlorvos, which is on the red list of dangerous chemicals – this list advises which chemicals should be avoided around human food products – is not totally successful as the lice develop a resistance to the chemicals fairly rapidly and, in any event, these are undesirable substances to introduce into a wild marine environment. Moreover, the sea-lice fall off and transfer to wild fish and depredation of wild stocks is said to occur. But I talked to Ori, an Icelandic businessman who has taken ten years off to save the wild Atlantic salmon, and he reckons netting at sea, the reckless taking of plankton to service the farmed industry and the banning of the seal cull have done more harm than transferred sea-lice to date. Since the banning of the seal cull, seal numbers have quadrupled. A seal will eat 500 lbs of fish a year, but even more disastrous than this is the seal's habit of taking a bite out of a fish and leaving the rest. In Nova Scotia – where there has been a moratorium on fishing certain banks for three years – fish stocks have not increased due to the huge number of seals. Seals will come right up a salmon river chasing the fish.

The problem of anaemia is more worrying for wild stocks. It is believed to have been carried on equipment transferred from Norway, and one major outbreak, with eleven subsidiary outbreaks, in 1995, ravaged the industry and caused losses of £37 million in destroyed stock. It is the BSE of salmon, although there is no evidence that it is transferable to humans. The farm I visited was one of the very few to escape, but Ray reckoned it would force the industry to clean up its act and take a long look at itself. Thirty-odd years is a very short space of time for any industry, and they have a long way to go and a lot to learn.

At the time of writing, however, I have discovered that Dr Jennie Mordue of Aberdeen University, where I am Rector – hurrah – is working on a three-year project to lure sea-lice away from the salmon and into traps. The idea is to use premones. Basically this is a sex-trap, rather like standing a superhooker by a lamppost to lure away a stalker. In this case the whore is replaced by a tethered turbot! It may sound wacky but it is far less insane than one suggestion, to feed carnivorous fish on vegetable matter. I spoke to Dr Mordue, who is very excited by the success of the project at this stage, and has invited me to the department. I love the thought of thousands of sexually over-excited sea-lice, so I shall be off like a shot! If she is successful, the savings to the fish-farming industry will be almost inestimable, to say nothing of the environmental implications.

Unfortunately, apart from anaemia and sea-lice, there is another big downside to salmon farming. The salmon are fed on pellets with a high oil content, which is why farmed salmon is much oilier than wild salmon. This, in turn, produces a runny faeces which travels much further than the usual faecal pellet. Salmon shit is high in ammonia, and the Scottish Growers Association do not dispute Friends of the Earth's figure which shows that 9,000 tons of untreated ammonia is released into the sea, each year, by fish farms. To my mind this means that the actual figure is probably higher. Added to this is the habit that many fish farmers have of pouring raw bleach into the pens in an attempt to kill sea-lice. Also, in reality, most salmon are not knocked on the head, but are fed cyanide pellets to kill them. They cannot be killed with an electric stunner because the supermarkets reject any bruised fish. It is an industry that badly needs regularizing before the seas are rendered sterile. The trouble is that farmed salmon prices are now so low that it has become a cut-throat industry.

Because salmon is so cheap we are returned to the days when the Edinburgh apprentices refused to eat it more than three times a week, and I, at last, have a use for all my historic recipes which are designed to make salmon more appealing to the jaded palate. There is, however, a place for salmon that isn't wild as a luxury product, and I am delighted to hear that a couple in Orkney are now farming the fish organically. When choosing farmed salmon, look for the colour: it should be a clear natural pink. Very red colouring is caused by chemicals, and very pale means insufficient plankton in the diet. If you see a white band of fat, it means that the fish has had insufficient exercise and, don't forget, the more muscular the tail the better.

I enjoyed my trip to the strange world of the fish farm. As my part of the story-line was that

Tobermory harbour

I would take away some salmon that I was supposed to have caught, I had to net some at the farm, which is not that easy. They were very heavy and Johnny wasn't fooled. But he never is!

I love the sea, and the sight of Tobermory harbour with its gaily painted houses lifted my heart. Such a strange name, it always makes me think of Saki's talking cat. I was raised on the tales of Para Handy and always look for the *Vital Spark* among any gathering of boats in Scotland. But the boats in this harbour were jaunty inshore fishing boats, and the one we were looking for belonged to a man by the nickname of Steptoe, I never did discover why. Highlanders are like Arabs, it is impossible to ask them a straight question and receive a straight answer: their minds are so complex. Unfortunately I forgot that, which is why I don't know why Steptoe is called Steptoe. Steptoe's boat was called the *Dawn Treader* and Johnny, the rotter, suggested his wife might be called Dawn. Steptoe and his twin brother both have prawn-fishing boats and they ply the waters of the Mull coast for several miles each side of Tobermory. Due to the weather we were unable to go past the harbour bar, and there was even a Para Handy-type Clyde puffer sheltering within the bar, unable to put out to sea for the weather. Steptoe told me that he has been caught out in many storms, and he seemed quite unfazed by the thought of sitting off a lee shore in a small fishing boat in a force ten gale. He fishes for prawns, or what you and I would call langoustines. They are caught in creels which are carefully baited and laid down in sets of thirty.

Steptoe works with a young man called Donald who wants to buy his own boat one day, an increasingly impossible prospect in the days of rising costs and falling stocks. It costs £60,000 for a licence and nearly £200,000 for a boat, which is a lot for a young man. Besides which fish stocks are falling and the best day will yield a maximum of 2 tons. Donald was baiting the traps with chunks of herring and I was surprised to discover that prawns, unlike crabs, like fresh bait. Apparently they will take salt fish but are not keen on rotten fish. The creels are reeled in on a winch run off the engine, a vast improvement on the hand-hauled creels I remember from holidays spent in the West of Ireland. When they were hauled in, the creels yielded their usual assortment of strange creatures, as well as the prawns. Johnny had a lovely time throwing small crabs back over the side. There were a lot of dogfish, strange sinister beasts with their threatening shark-like eyes and long sinuous bodies. We prudently saved some in a bucket for the fishing sequence on Craignure pier planned for that evening, in case we failed to catch any for the camera.

The ban on scallop fishing had been lifted that day and I talked to Steptoe about that industry. Due to toxins found in scallops – discovered some eight months earlier – a ban had been imposed to allow the scallops time to clean themselves. The main blame seems to fall on the salmon farmers for (it is alleged) introducing the toxin ASP from its waste into the sea. This toxin, when it enters the human system, causes nausea, dizziness, vomiting, possible brain damage and even death. The scallop industry, which harvested 46 tons of queen scallops and 27 tons of king scallops in 1997, has been hard hit. Scallops are a major source of income, worth more than £17 million annually, but no compensation has been paid to scallop fishermen and the fear is that other shellfish may be contaminated. The boats have had to turn to other fish crops for a living, but there isn't much of a market for white fish. The fishermen blame pollution from the fish farms for the problem, although this is a close-knit community with everyone striving to make what living they can from the island's resources. There was a more *laissez-faire* attitude between the different sections of the community than I had anticipated. Time and again I got the feeling that the Islanders enjoyed the challenge of ringing the changes from their environment, whether they be tourists, deer, salmon, timber or the gifts of the sea: they were all crops to be harvested.

The prawns were fine lively specimens, some of them up to eight inches long, and they can give you quite a nip. There was a good catch as Steptoe hadn't fished inside the bar for a while. The prawns were boxed up and kept in the cooler until they were collected and transported south. This industry is a huge export industry: 34,085 tons are caught each year and most go abroad. Two months earlier I had been eating Scottish prawns on the south coast of Spain. It is one of those mysteries of the food industry that one can seldom buy locally caught seafood, and almost never in restaurants. Supermarkets buy imported fish and seafood, spending £13.5 million a year on imported cod and only £4 million on home-caught fish, with other seafood running at about 75%, or more, as imported purchases. However, the prawns we took with us to cook on our beach bonfire in the pouring rain were delicious.

ABOVE: The prawn catch
BELOW: Cooking prawns on a very wet beach barbecue

For me one of the real treats of this adventure was visiting the Reeds, who make Isle of Mull Cheddar. This was a particular request of mine as I have long been a fan of this hand-crafted cheese which never has a murky flavour: you can taste the seasons in the unpasturized milk. The family moved up from Somerset twenty years before to follow a dream. Many are lured by the idea of a *Good Life* existence in the West Highlands but find the hard conditions and the isolation too much and slink back with their tails between their legs. The Reed family, however, were made of hardier stuff. With true pioneering spirit they, and their young sons, rebuilt the farm from a ruined shell. When they started, with five cows, they used to make the cheese in a bucket. Today they have thirty Friesians which they milk three times a day. The milk is transferred straight from the cooling tanks to the cheese vats where the rennet is added.

Despite the warm and genuine hospitality of the Reeds, one eye was always on the clock as the curds will spoil if left for a fraction too long. I found myself clad in a long rubber apron and mob cap, cutting the curds with a long-handled tool which is held vertically and moved to and fro through the setting curds. It is harder than it looks. Chris Reed told me that they once had a girl to stay who insisted on bathing in the whey and, as she was rather good looking, the sons willingly carried up buckets daily! The curds were pleasantly warm, and had a silky sensuous feel as you ran a hand through them to ensure they were breaking into small enough pieces. The whey is then drained off and the curds are salted and left to cheddar before being packed into presses and put under pressure.

At this point Johnny joined us, fragrant from shit-shovelling in the milking shed, and looking particularly fetching in his apron, although he insisted on wearing his beloved old tweed cap and refused a mob. The farm uses old hand presses with 100 lb weights and, once pressed, the cheeses are turned out and ironed. The intention at every stage is to improve the rind and Chris is experimenting with ironing the rims with a domestic iron: the smell of toasting cheese was mouth-watering. Johnny and I then helped bandage the cheese. This is a laborious and painstaking task reminiscent of first-aid classes. The bandages must be well greased and smoothed onto the cheese with no gaps or air bubbles, or the cheese may spoil. The mould then forms on the bandages, not on the cheese.

The cheeses are surprisingly heavy and Johnny, who is tough as old boots, and used to chucking ewes over each shoulder and striding down the hill, was taken aback. Chris, with years of experience, handled them as if they were featherdown,

ABOVE: Cheese harvest
OPPOSITE TOP: Singing in the rain
OPPOSITE BELOW: Cutting the curds

tossing them over with one hand. When wrapped, the cheeses are carried by hand over to the cheese cellar where they are stored on slate shelves and left to mature for between ten months and a year. It was a beautiful sight: hundreds of cheeses made from thousands of man-hours and gallons of milk, all waiting patiently to become perfect.

We went back to the milking shed for the next round. I stuck the milking unit on the cow's teats, ignoring the various unprintable comments from Johnny, and as the milk poured into the bucket I reflected on this strange conversion of grass to cheese, and wondered how it ever began in the first place. No wonder farmers are so philosophical.

Dodging the shit, Johnny was all for converting it to methane gas for use as a natural source of power. He also suggested that the ideal conversion chamber was the Millennium Dome ... make of that what you will, dear reader!

CHAPTER FOUR

A FLAT CAP, GREYHOUND SHIT AND PIGEON DUNG

J The recommended procedure after a week's filming is to sit in a darkened room for a day, preferably with an understanding dog, and let the adrenaline seep out. Our feet touched the ground running after Mull. There were five days before filming the next programme, work to do on the synopsis and an incredible number of contributors to telephone. The morning after I returned to the bosom of my family and should have been groping blindly for normality, Clarissa arrived carrying her laptop.

'Right,' she said, 'you telephone, I'll type.'

The majority of the material for the programmes was being provided by us, and it was a condition of our involvement that where field sports were concerned the initial approach would always be made by us. The purpose of programme three was to portray how those, whose lot it is to live in cities, are still able to be involved in and take an active part in field sports. 'A flat cap, greyhound shit and pigeon dung' was a music-hall joke describing the urban sportsman at the turn of the century. We wanted to show that his grandson was alive and well, and just as sporting, in the millennium. We filmed ferreting, pigeon racing, coursing under National Coursing Club rules and the blue riband of coursing, the Waterloo Cup. We have to thank Lord Leverhulme, the keepers on his estate at Altcar and the members of the Cup Committee for all their help and support.

Coursing is the oldest of all field sports, dating back to the Pharaohs, and greyhounds are a breed of great antiquity. When hunting was the primary method of filling a larder, greyhounds were the most prized of all the hounds in a nobleman's kennels. Matching the speed, skill and stamina of two greyhounds against a hare, the fastest and most agile of all creatures, is an ancient pastime. The Romans were mad keen on their coursing and imported the brown hare into Britain so that they could continue their sport here. The earliest recording of the ethos of match coursing, upon which the National Coursing Club rules are based, are in the writings of Arrian, a Roman living in the first century AD. 'The aim of the true sportsman with hounds is not to take the hare, but to engage her in a racing contest, or duel, and he is pleased if she escapes.'

What was true then is equally true today, and the strict rules of the NCC include the important decision to impose a closed season for hares. This runs between 11 March and 14 September.

Coursing under NCC rules is possibly the most maligned and least understood of all field sports. It is also the only one where the object is not to kill the quarry. Hares are very territorial and, if disturbed, will run in a wide circle back to their form. At a driven coursing meeting, beaters slowly bring in a large area of land towards the running ground, selected so that hares naturally cross it as part of the route back to their own ground. Flankers guide hares into a field, usually ploughed, at the bottom end of the running ground, where they are able to rest. As numbers build up, the first ones into the field, having had a breather, follow their natural instinct and break for the open. Fifty yards in front of the plough is a canvas shy where the slipper is waiting with the two greyhounds competing in that course. The slipper, a trained official licensed by the NCC, has enormous responsibilities. He must decide whether the hare is fit to course. Probably only one third that come on to a running ground will actually be coursed.

Hares should pass within thirty yards of the shy and be moving straight. They are given a lead of never less than eighty yards. Satisfied that the hare is fit, the slipper runs forward with the dogs, and once both are sighted, releases the catch holding the double collars and the course is on. The average course lasts thirty seconds and is an incredible display of speed. A hare has 80% rear vision and is capable of turning in its own length without losing speed. A mounted judge awards points for, in simplistic terms, speed and ability to make the hare turn. Each dog wears a red or white knitted collar and the winner is identified by the judge waving a red or white handkerchief. The coursing ground will have, as its boundary, either a hedge or a drainage canal. At various intervals are soughs, artificially constructed underground refuges.

Greyhounds, like salukis, borzois, whippets and deer-hounds are one of the breed known as

The run up

gaze-hounds: they hunt entirely by sight. A hare need only disappear from view for a second for the greyhound to become 'unsighted', lose interest and stop coursing. All greyhounds running at coursing meetings under NCC rules have to be registered in a Stud Book established in 1882.

Clarissa was getting stronger by the day. Eight weeks after major surgery she had made two programmes requiring colossal physical and mental input, and we were setting off for the next one with no form of break between filming. As we thundered down the motorway, she said for the third time since Christmas, 'We're off Johnny, on another adventure.' We arrived, as usual after our long journeys, weak with laughter. The following day, we filmed the greyhounds at Johnnie O'Shea's kennels. Our syndicate had three greyhounds in training and two pups coming on. We then went to a nearby field to film Tom, our Cup hopeful and winner of the Scottish National, being trained to the lure. As Tom streaked off in pursuit of the lure I thought how exactly he conformed with Dame Juliana Berner's definition of the perfect greyhound – the head of a snake, neck of a drake, foot of a cat, tail of a rat, side of a bream and back like a beam, and all the qualities of speed, stamina, bravery and fire. The old girl knew what she was on about when she wrote her *Boke of St Albans* in the fifteenth century.

The training of any athlete, animal or human, is a highly skilled and dedicated art. Johnnie O'Shea is among the growing number of ex Hunt Servants who have become successful trainers, giving us a number of winners and two runners in the Waterloo Cup since the syndicate was formed. That afternoon we went to see Sam Bell, Lord Leverhulme's Head Keeper at Altcar, home of the Waterloo Cup. Match coursing became regularized at much the same time as hunting was developing along the lines we know it today. Lord Orford started the first club, the Swaffham Coursing Society, in 1776 and laid down rules, based loosely on Elizabethan ones. The new sport became spectacularly popular and within a quarter of a century there were organized coursing meetings all over the country. The Altcar Club was formed by Lord Molyneux who later became the Earl of Sefton in 1825. Eleven years later, William Lynn, the famous sporting hotelier at whose establishment, the Waterloo Hotel, club members habitually dined before meetings, asked permission to hold a meeting of his own. Lynn won his own stake and named the event after his hotel. He had recently built a two-mile steeplechase circuit at Aintree complete with grandstand, and decided to offer spectators a sporting package of coursing and steeplechasing.

The Waterloo Cup became a sixteen-dog stake in 1837, doubled again the following year and eventually ended up as a sixty-four-dog stake in 1857. Soon the Cup was attracting enormous numbers and, by the turn of the century, spectators exceeded 100,000 and the prize money was equal to a Derby winner's. Coursing featured in advertisements – for example Black and White whisky – and coursing memorabilia was distributed in shops in exchange for coupons accumulated with the purchase of certain products. News of the Cup winner was telegraphed to the Stock Exchange, and in John Buchan's *The Thirty-Nine Steps*, when Mr Memory is asked who won the Cup, his questioner refers to the Waterloo Cup, not the FA Cup. But two world wars, and the growing popularity of track racing, with its comparative comfort and convenience, saw numbers drop away. The Seventies were a sad period for the brown hare, coursing and the Waterloo Cup. The mania for agricultural productivity and monoculture dramatically reduced

Suncrest Tina

the hare population, wild partridges and many little songbirds, as their habitat and food source was destroyed. Lord Sefton died without an heir and 147 years of family patronage ended. With fewer and fewer hares the Cup struggled to exist at all.

It did continue to exist thanks to a small band of diehards, in particular Sir Mark Prescott, Bt, who were determined to keep the Cup going, and to the incredible good fortune that Lord Leverhulme, a lifelong friend of Lord Sefton, bought the Altcar estate. Anxious to see the Waterloo Cup continue, he has given the committee every assistance. With the future of the Cup assured, and the introduction of careful conservation methods, hares began to increase on land where farmers and landlords supported coursing under NCC rules. Poachers were becoming a major problem and, without the incentive to conserve hares for coursing, the simplest method of getting rid of the poachers was to get rid of the hares.

With farming methods sympathetic to hare conservation, a mix of arable grass and root crops, the hare population at Altcar is thriving. Unfortunately here, and in other areas where the hare population has expanded, landowners and farmers are under attack from organized gangs of poachers, who kill hares with lurchers. These are not old-fashioned pot hunters but extremely unpleasant and often dangerous thugs. Sam Bell and his under-keepers are continually occupied trying to keep them out.

The town of Southport is to the Waterloo Cup what Newmarket is to raceweek. Every hotel and boarding house is booked well in advance, and Little Blackpool suddenly looks like Olympia when Smithfield is on: lots of tweed and brick-red faces. The Cup really starts with the 'Call Over' on the evening before the first day, when the magnificent trophies for the Cup are displayed in the ballroom of the Scarisbroke Hotel. By now the Irish contingent have arrived and there is standing room only in the ballroom. 'Sweaty, smoky, but lots of fun!' as someone described it. Mark Prescott calls out the names of the dogs. Charles Blanning gives a précis of each one's form and Stephen Little, who sponsors the Cup, dickers over the odds with Alex Smith and Bernard Barry from Ireland, the principal bookies. There is a tremendous build-up of atmosphere and excitement for the forthcoming three days.

The first day of the Cup is always at the Withins, a coursing ground which favours dogs whose prowess is speed, with hares making a beeline for the soughs at the far end of the ground. Lydiate is more for a dog that is agile and can work. A Cup winner needs to be able to do both. Unusually, the weather was beautiful. I had anticipated, at best, driving rain. The crew filmed the stream of buses and cars driving on to the field, the bookies setting up, Johnnie O'Shea arriving with Tom, upon whom our syndicate's hopes were pinned, and the other trainers walking their dogs. They filmed the banks filling up with the thousands of spectators who come out from Liverpool and the surrounding countryside.

Clarissa and I nearly didn't make it. As we were driving from Southport to Altcar the gearstick

The bank

on the Land Rover surprised us both by becoming detached. Equally surprisingly, when I rammed it forcibly back in, it remained there perfectly happily, showing no further inclination to part company with the rest of the gearbox. When we arrived we parked the Land Rover in the trainers' car park, having thought up the clever idea of Clarissa handing out bacon butties to people we wanted to film: Garry Kelly the slipper, Bob Burden the judge and various trainers. Coursing enthusiasts Tariq and his cousins joined us and, because they do not eat bacon, Clarissa cooked them eggs.

Shortly before 9.30 am, as the first dogs moved up to the slips, Robin repositioned himself amongst the crowd by the bookies. Morning Brew and Suncrest Tina were slipped onto a strong straight running hare soon after 9.30 am, and the 164th Waterloo Cup was under way. Tom, and the dog he was to run against, Only Mover, both at 50–1, were seventeenth into slips, so Robin filmed Clarissa and me ambling about doing what we would normally do at the Cup: greeting friends, nattering to people and having the odd punt with Stephen Little who was, as always, the picture of sartorial practicality in his great-grandmother's fur coat and a pair of Second World War flying boots. Esmé and Shu were down at the far end of the running ground where the hares disappear into the shelter of the rough ground, soughs and rhododendron bushes. Steve discussed the form with Tariq and it was, to all intents and purposes, another magical Cup day.

The mixture of people from all walks of life who come coursing is a fine example of how field sports create an intimacy between those at opposite ends of the social scale. The cross-section of society that gathers for the Waterloo Cup is extraordinary. It is, to my mind, one of the particular charms of the Cup. In any other circumstances you would never expect to see such diverse groups of people deep in conversation with each other. Take away the trappings of modern life and there is an almost Regency air about the whole event.

Sadly our syndicate dog, Tom, was beaten. It was a big disappointment for us and for the crew, all of whom, we were touched and embarrassed to discover, had sneaked off individually and placed bets on him. At midday there is a break as the beat comes in and the antis were escorted by mounted police on to the ground and then penned up on the road between the nominators' and trainers' car parks. Clarissa and I walked across the nominators' car park to talk to some of the syndicate members. In the last couple of years, with increased media attention, some animal welfare groups have issued instructions that their more violent and extreme element have to save their activities for Southport in the evening and to behave themselves at the Cup. This year's lot were much the same as any. One or two old things who thoroughly disapprove of battery-reared chickens, a lot of students wearing Balaclavas so that mummy won't recognize them if they happen to be televised and the nasty element that gets them all to swear and shout.

Normally you can't hear much of what they shout because there is a howling wind blowing straight off the Irish Sea at them, but this year we could hear quite distinctly, above the invective, a croaking voice chanting, 'One fat lady's dead. One to go.' It was sickening and it horrified us all. Clarissa turned four-square and stared into the crowd. I could not decide whether the owner of the voice was a man or a woman, but how anyone could radiate such hate was beyond me. Finally, with reluctance and great dignity, Clarissa walked slowly back to the Land Rover, visibly shaken.

As we were leaving for Southport I spotted young Ensign Dolby, one of our syndicate members. Piers Dolby, for it was he, had obviously fallen in with bad companions during the day and was currently being taught the intricacies of an Irish jig by Mickey Flanagan, and Mickey's village priest, who always comes with him to the Cup. Now there is nothing unusual in the sight of an officer in the 5th Foot Guards dancing in a muddy puddle with a portly Roman Catholic priest, and a small flushed ex-Hunt Servant, at the end of the first day. What did strike me as odd, having not seen him earlier, was that Piers Dolby and Vinnie Faal – a very vocal member of the Countryside Alliance – evidently shared the same taste in loud tweed. Not only that, but each had persuaded a hatter to make them headwear from the same material, in the style of a 1920s motoring cap. From a distance, the two would have been indistinguishable.

The vicinity of the Scarisbroke Hotel is made dangerous by the antis. The previous year Garry

Kelly was in his car when a mob almost wrecked it, and two old ladies who had ventured into a side street had been brutally attacked. On our return Southport was buzzing with the news that Vinnie Faal had been arrested. Having business at the Scarisbroke, he had notified the police outside the Prince of Wales Hotel, where he was staying, that he, Andrew Pilkington of *The Countryman's Weekly*, Vinnie's young son Rory and a seventy-year-old solicitor (and veteran of the Welsh march) could expect to be targeted by the antis. They asked for protection. Even so they had been pelted with eggs and, as they made a run for the police cordon, a breakaway flying picket of antis had attacked them. Vinnie threw his arms up to protect himself as a woman leapt onto his back. She fell to the ground unhurt, but Vinnie was arrested for the offence of 'threatening words and behaviour.'

I met Vinnie's wife, Lesley, at the Scarisbroke and offered to go down to the police station and find out when Vinnie was likely to be released. There was not an anti in sight, which was an eerie feeling because I knew they were somewhere in the side streets. Fifty yards from the Scarisbroke I suddenly heard shrieking voices howling, 'Vinnie Faal, Vinnie Faal.' Looking back I saw a mêlée of khaki-clad figures dancing and darting round a car drawn up outside the hotel. The police were struggling to help the occupants and in the middle of it all was the unmistakable sight of Vinnie's cap. He must be out on bail already, I thought. Side-stepping a police horse and a woman with pupils the size of pinheads, I shot into the foyer. In the confusion Vinnie appeared to be wrestling with a large policeman. 'Hoy,' he said, 'get your hands off me. I'm an Officer in the Brigade of Guards.' I instantly recognized the voice and smiled to myself. It was Piers Dolby. The antis had got the wrong man. The prosecution, by the way, subsequently dropped their case against Vinnie Faal.

The second day at the Lydiate is a real test of skill and agility. Dogs that have come through the first round of the Cup because of their speed, now have to prove equal prowess on hares that twist and turn as they seek the refuge of the soughs. The committee had kindly agreed to allow us to film with the beaters. Clarissa and I had a bet and were slightly up on the first day. I decided to use this to set up a betting syndicate for the crew in the hope of winning back some of their losses on Tom. Before leaving I had a long confab with Tariq and his cousin Mo who knew the form. I placed a series of bets with Stephen Little.

We joined Sam Bell and the beaters lined out along the top end of the road onto the Lydiate. Robin set the camera up. Sam spoke into his radio and the beaters advanced at an incredible speed across a ploughed field, while the crew struggled to keep up. Mercifully, after the first field, the beat slowed considerably, with frequent stops, and Robin was able to film. It was a fascinating experience for me. Over sixty beaters are involved, formed into two separate lines which eventually join as they come in towards the running ground where the hares are guided towards the slipper by about twenty flankers. Spaced on either side of the running ground are four hare dispatchers

Tariq and family

ready to dispose of a hare humanely in the event of one being caught. There are also a considerable number of marshals, officials and security guards.

Sam was constantly on the radio to his under-keepers, stopping the line to let hares move ahead naturally. Unfortunately a gang of poachers appeared on the opposite bank of the canal that runs along the left of the fields approaching the running ground. They were killing hares as they broke over the bridge or swam across the canal. This, coupled with a strong wind in our faces, drove a lot of hares back through the line.

Clarissa had spent a jolly morning being interviewed by the media, gassing to mates and shrewdly placing long odds. By the end of the day the betting syndicate was well forward. The third day was one of quite astonishing excitement. Not only was it my birthday but the betting syndicate was looking healthy and the favourite, Grisham, upon whom I had staked our winnings, looked like a dead cert. The opening semi-final was thrilling. Grisham led by almost two lengths against Suncrest Tina, who suddenly started to motor. What a course: just managing to drive herself past Grisham, Suncrest Tina gained the turn and never looked back. Although down to our original stake, we were delighted for the dog's owners.

Next into slips were Twins Ballerina and our old friend Terry Connor's Minstrel Black, the bravest dog at the Cup. After an enormously gruelling course Minstrel Black was through to the final. In the break in the proceedings we placed the remainder of our original stake. Minstrel Black was heavily handicapped after his course, but even so I put my chemise and moral support on him. Clarissa, who is less of a sentimentalist, plunged on Suncrest Tina.

We also met some American coursing fanatics, through Audrey Trotti, a stunning American PhD student at York University. They have dogs in training over there where they course jackrabbits, under similar rules. We interviewed these people as the final was being run. Huge odds were stacked against Minstrel Black; his earlier courses, in the run-up to the semi-final, had been real workers. A huge roar went up in support of a dog that exemplified all the qualities of courage that centuries of breeding had created. But his best was not good enough, and Suncrest Tina won the Millennium Waterloo Cup at which, as usual, fewer than ten hares had been killed.

It had been an absolutely magical three days. Whatever the crew may have thought of it all, they had clearly enjoyed being part of the excitement. As we were leaving we bumped into our old friend, Uncouth Keith, resplendent in greasy leather cap and gold earrings. Keith uses the word Miranda to describe something wonderful. A lottery win would be Miranda to him, or the first pint of the day. 'Would you describe me as Miranda?' Clarissa asked him coyly. Her win on Tina had made her a tad light-headed.

'Noo', said Keith. 'I would describe you, Clarissa, as the goddess of wet dreams!'

A postscript, but an important one, to our visit to the Waterloo Cup, is that afterwards we went to Birmingham to film Tariq – who met us earlier and discussed form. He took us to meet his brother, Mohamed. We knew that many Pakistanis were coursing enthusiasts and Johnny had wanted to track some of them down and enlist their support for the London march. Johnny describes himself as a hunter-gatherer and his attitude to facts he wishes to acquire, or people he wants to find, has a quality reminiscent of a terrier at a hole. Despite much relentless pursuit he failed to find them in time for the march but, just before we were due to film the coursing programme, the phone rang and with that happy whoop that I have heard so often down the years he announced that he'd found some people who were willing to take part in the programme. The trouble had been that when he was trying to find them the coursing season had not begun, so he couldn't track them down at a meeting, and because it is customary among the Pakistani community to live in multi-family households, letters can sometimes go astray due to the similarity of names. Also, those with the best English go out to work, so telephone calls can be a fruitless exercise. Johnny had eventually managed to track them down when he heard that one of the community had won a major coursing prize at Swaffham.

We filmed Mohamed in a terraced house in a room hung with Islamic scriptural texts. He sat in front of a formidable tier of coursing cups inscribed in English or Urdu, and he gave us a video of coursing in Pakistan. In Pakistan hare coursing, which is mostly park coursing, is the single

'Do you know where Tariq lives?'

largest sport and they import between 60 and 100 dogs each year from the British Isles or the Republic of Ireland. The family love the sport and one of the cousins told me he had had great emotional difficulties when he came to England. He had been very depressed and it was only his involvement with the dogs that had saved his sanity. Can you imagine any other circumstances in which such information would be shared between a man and a woman who were total strangers and from such disparate backgrounds?

The family live in the middle of Birmingham and they train their dogs by walking them, four times a day, round the one-mile circumference of the local park. The walking is done by the younger members of the family and it was splendid to see quite young boys proudly walking the greyhounds in their care. In order to train them to the lure, they have to get up and go to the park at first light, before there any other distractions about. This is a sign of their dedication to the sport: this is a family of true urban sportsmen. Their park-trained dogs are the winners of the cups we saw with Mohamed.

I remembered a headline in the *Daily Record* on an article about coursing. It read: 'Toffs get their rocks off'. The article writer was obviously not particularly well informed about the great mixture of people who train dogs and go coursing. Many field sports create bonds between people of quite different cultures and classes, and coursing is a particularly good example of this. While we were waiting to film a sequence in a Balti restaurant in Sparkbrooke, I watched Tariq, the

Pakistani baker, and Johnny, the English sheep farmer, both men with a natural reserve, nattering over a form book like two old school friends, happy as Larry.

The point, which will not have escaped you, dear reader, is to illustrate the wide variety of people who come together to enjoy field sports and the camaraderie that naturally springs up between them. Although it is true that one seldom comes across people of colour in the country – there is a black MFH in the New Forest, but he does not represent the norm – there is no doubt that people of all backgrounds are welcomed by those who farm and take part in field sports. This might serve to counter IFAW's charge, levelled at the Countryside Alliance marchers in 1997, that country people are racist. It simply isn't true.

After coursing, we went ferreting. The philosophy behind this particular programme was somewhat different from the others because we were attempting to illustrate what the urban man does for sport in the countryside. One of the obvious choices was ferreting. I am aware that in allowing me to write this section of the book Johnny is engaging in an act of true friendship. Ferrets are Johnny's thing. Ever since I can remember he has seldom been without one. His great party trick, when we were children, was to put his little jill ferret up one sleeve of his jacket and we would watch, fascinated, as the bump travelled up his arm, across his shoulders and emerged from the other sleeve. This trick nearly ended in tears when, one hot day, Johnny's ferret, smelling the blood below the skin, started digging into his armpit to find the vein!

It would be difficult to know more about ferrets than Johnny does, so be grateful that he has made this supreme sacrifice, for I know for a fact that his lifetime ambition is a twenty-one-volume work on ferrets – if he can condense it into so short a space – the fifty-volume unexpurgated edition will be available on limited subscription only! This puts a great responsibility on me and I am aware of the sword of Damocles hanging over my head as I write. Because Johnny has no ferrets at present, we persuaded Vinnie Faal's son, Rory, who keeps ferrets in a rather splendid caged area in the garden, to take us ferreting.

My polecat and albino ferrets, 1966

The ancestry of the ferret is uncertain: of the potential candidates the marbled polecat is virtually ruled out by skull shape. The favoured candidates are the European polecat, or foulmart, and the Asiatic or Steppe polecat. Incidentally a sweetmart is a pine marten: the names refer to the scent of their respective dung. Modern research has favoured the Steppe polecat as the original basic genetic material for the modern ferret, but both contenders have fierce followings. Originally the ferret was used to hunt sousliks – Steppe marmosets and hamsters – for food. Now the ferret is a vital tool for netting rabbits, whether used by a poacher or a keeper. Keeping ferrets is, by the way, not considered evidence of poaching because their other use is clearing rats from barns and houses.

Argument rages as to whether it was the Romans or the Normans who brought the rabbit to England. I favour the latter, for there is no doubt that by Plantagenet times each estate had its own warren as part of the living larder system and names such as de Warenne, or Warrender, are evidence of this. Had the Romans brought them here one thousand years earlier, I am sure there would have been more evidence of this in Saxon writings. Warren rabbits were kept in semi-captivity as a food source and, in England, they belonged to the owner of the land and it was a crime to hunt them – not so now.

We set out with Rory, his ferrets and his lurcher and Pilk (Andrew Pilkington) with his Bedlington-cross lurcher called Red. In any field there are always a number of burrows, most of which will be empty, so the lurchers are used to suss out which ones contain rabbits and should therefore be ferreted. It was a pretty sight to see the lurchers bounding through the standing game crop of sunflowers – which had been planted as a headland of cover for pheasants – leaping straight-legged with ears pricked. When a suitable burrow is chosen, it is vital to net all the holes because you can bet heavily that the rabbit will escape through the one open one. The nets are short nets – I like the old-fashioned ones made of sisal but the newer plastic ones don't tangle so easily when wet. The ferret is sent down the hole and a new gadget, the electronic ferret locator, means that if the ferret gets stuck underground you can find it quickly and dig it out, thus saving hours of waiting. The ferret's shuffling movement, coupled with its short forward spurt, is perfect for latching onto rabbits underground, but usually the rabbit will bolt into the net, where a quick twist of the neck provides a speedy dispatch and a tasty meal. Sadly our borrows proved virtually empty, though we did net a couple, thus proving once again that field sports are about patience and skill and not bloodlust.

When country people moved to the towns, with the coming of the Industrial Revolution, they took their ferrets with them. Ferrets don't take up much room and are easy to keep, if basic rules of hygiene are observed. Moreover the country was much nearer to the town before the suburbs intervened, and rabbits had become a nuisance, so landowners were willing to give permission for their removal. People like Rory still keep ferrets in towns and the final shot in this sequence is of Lesley Faal cooking the rabbits we had caught and remarking that, in really hard times, they had existed on the creatures: she had made rabbit hamburgers and rabbit bolognese for the children. In the Midlands, in particular, the old tradition of a coney for the pot still strongly survives.

Albino ferret tangled in flan net

The other great urban sport is pigeon racing. The domestication of the rock-dove, as part of the living larder system, is as old as time. Near Cairo in Egypt you can see a huge cliff face, hand-hewn with pigeon-holes dating from before the pyramids. They are still filled with the birds, and still supply squab for a well-known nearby restaurant which only serves pigeons. The wood pigeon, *Columba palumbus*, also known as the ring-dove, is the largest European dove. It grows up to 16 inches (40 centimetres) and is the best eating. The British Isles abound with old dovecots and where I live the house was built, in 1748, complete with a brand new dovecot: proof that even fashionable people were still using this resource then.

Today we are faced with the ridiculous situation that restaurateurs buy imported squab, young pigeon from Europe, and even America, whilst thousands of fine dovecots stand empty, or provide homes for ornamental doves. A squab is a four-week-old bird which is still at the fledgling stage. Once pigeons leave the nest they quickly become tough. Commercial squabs are raised from the *Columba livia* strain which is descended from the rock-doves; they weigh between 8 and 14 oz. One of the main reasons that pigeons are such a prolific food resource is that they breed the entire year round, and it is this propensity which has led to their other great usage: as homing birds and message-carriers. If you separate a pigeon from its mate, it becomes very frustrated and will display amazing skills to return to her.

How this was first discovered is a mystery, but we do know that pigeons have been used as message-carriers by the military, and by shrewd financiers, since ancient Egyptian times. Pliny was a keen pigeon-fancier and wrote eloquently about their use. One of my own favourite stories is about how the Rothschild family arranged for a pigeon to be sent from the battlefield at Waterloo. On learning of Wellington's overwhelming victory they spread word that the French had won, and attempted a monumental coup on the London Stock Exchange. This was only thwarted by a Yorkshireman called Sam Buller who, declaring, 'I don't believe them demned Frenchies have us beat', bought stocks valiantly. In both world wars pigeons saved thousands of lives, sending messages from the front, or recording the location of downed aircraft. Of the fifty-three Dickin Medals – known as the animals' VC – awarded for bravery, thirty-one have gone to pigeons.

The sport of pigeon racing developed with the railways. In order for your pigeon to be sent far enough away to make its race home interesting, you need a mode of transport that will make its outward journey quick and stress free (I can't believe I just said that about rail travel, but it was quicker and more efficient then). In 1897 the sport became organized with the formation of the Royal Pigeon Racing Association (RPRA) based at Leeds. They are now based midway between Cheltenham and Gloucester. The Patron of the Association is Her Majesty the Queen, apparently a keen pigeon-fancier herself. The membership of the Association ranges from peers to professionals to the traditional flat-capped heartland members. Over 75,000 members actively race pigeons throughout the British Isles and Gibraltar, with 3,000 racing clubs. Worldwide supporters number over 1,000,000: the sport has spread from America to Pakistan to the Antipodes.

We went to see a pigeon-racer called Tommy in his pigeon-loft which is attached to his house, near Manchester. Tommy's forebears have been involved in the sport since his great-grandfather's day, and he is a passionate enthusiast. He explained how the sport works. Every year the RPRA issues about one and a half million new leg-rings for the current year's crop. Each pigeon is registered, by number, at six days old. There is a special clock, obtained from the club and this records the starting time of each pigeon. This is usually done at the club, and the birds are loaded onto lorries and taken to the starting point where they are released simultaneously. A rubber race-ring, with a capsule attached, is fixed to each bird's leg before the race. When the pigeon lands back in the loft the capsule is immediately passed into the clock which records the arrival time. Seconds are vital and the existence of the pigeon-loft discourages birds from hanging around on rooftops, and lures them straight back to their mate, where water and food also await the homing pigeon, thus enabling the speediest registration.

The distance raced ranges from a minimum of 60 miles, increasing to 200 miles for young birds and 500 miles for old ones. The pigeon flying the greatest number of yards per minute wins, and nowadays the exact distance from start point to each competing member's home loft is calculated by computer, thereby avoiding some of the rows which once shook the sport. The speeds are astonishing and there have been times recorded well in excess of 2,000 yards per minute.

Before the race

Tommy's loft was beautifully kept, clean and airy. The competitive birds live in the racing loft with their mates in cages which are cleverly constructed so that they can be together and separate, rather like an Edwardian husband who was banished to the dressing-room to build up his sexual frustration. There was also a loft for the breeding stock which included one incredibly old, but still active, bird aged twenty-four. His beak curled over like a mandarin's fingernail and needed repeated trimming. There was also a separate area where the birds sat on, and hatched, their eggs in the traditional clay pots which smacked of ancient Rome. Both birds sit on the eggs (which I remembered are a great delicacy in China) and become very fierce if you come too close. As Tommy moved one aside to show us the ugly yellow chicks, the hen pecked angrily at his finger.

The price of birds ranges from £20 to an astonishing £106,000 for a breeding cock. The main danger to racing pigeons are raptors: sparrowhawks and peregrine falcons take out pigeons in astonishing numbers. In the summer a strategically placed peregrine falcon lives on nothing else. This is distressing and expensive for the owners, and unamusing for the sport. Since the Royal Society for the Protection of Birds forced through legislation to prevent the culling of raptors, the situation has become much worse, with 60% of Scottish racing birds taken out crossing the Border Hills. About 6,000 racing pigeons a year are taken out by hawks and we were able to see, firsthand, the anguish it causes.

Part of the story-line for this part of the programme was that as the racing season had not yet begun, but the birds were out of moult, Tommy was to arrange a private race for us. The

BBC devised a story-line whereby, in order to cheat on the bet, I surreptitiously wrote my name on both racing-rings so that I would win either way. This jolly exercise nearly turned very sour. The birds were taken off by a friend of Tommy and released five miles away. Tommy, Johnny and I paced the yard watching the sky and the tension grew. There were a number of feral pigeons about, which would lift the heart momentarily; it was surprisingly exciting.

Tommy remarked that there was a hawk about; he could tell this from the movement of the wild birds. I felt a cold finger trace my spine. One bird came back with a flurry and was scooped up,

The tearful return

de-race-ringed and put back with its mate where he preened happily at the fuss she made of his return – humans could learn a lot from pigeons. We waited back in the yard but the second bird did not appear, and dread joined our group.

Tommy was very brave and I wanted to hug him for his distress, and his courage in not showing it. He talked of squalls, rain showers and freak gusts of winds, and we all tried to perform for the camera. But it became obvious that the bird was not going to return and, with heavy hearts, we filmed an ending, packed up our gear and left, shaking hands with an anguished Tommy. However his friend, Len, was optimistic, but no one believed him.

Johnny and I climbed into the Land Rover and Steve decided to film a leaving shot. Just as we started the engine, Len ran out crying that the bird was home, so Robin scooped up the camera and we rushed back. Tommy was nearly in tears and lacrimose old me was weeping openly. Even Johnny was moved: you can tell by a tightening of the eyes if you know what to look for.

The bird had been attacked by the hawk and escaped, and Tommy showed us the damaged pin-feathers which, thankfully, will grow back. We filmed the Hollywood ending and left again. This time Tommy and I hugged each other with real feeling. It brought home to me how dreadful the suspense of waiting for a pigeon to return must be for the competitors, and how they worry that their pigeons will be killed by raptors. What a strange world it has become when misinformed politicians, and uncomprehending Townies, upset the balance of nature by protecting vermin to the detriment of field sports and to nature herself.

THE BALLAD OF THE OLD RED QUAD-BIKE

J Hunting, dearie me, the one all the fuss is about. The one Tony Blair has stubbed his toe on and the one that will astonish future students of Scottish political history. Let us have a shufti at what is at stake. There are 312 registered hound packs in the British Isles covering 150,000 square miles of hunting country. The majority of Hunts own their own property, facilities and equipment. Their inventory includes in excess of 300 kennels and stabling, 150 flesh houses and incinerators. About 400 houses and flats provide accommodation for Hunt staff and there are over 6,500 acres of covert and over 1,500 acres of paddock.

They own more than 250 lorries, 200 trucks and pick-ups and over 20 quad-bikes; nearly 950 hunters worth the best part of £2 million; some 8,000 couple of entered hounds and over 2,000 un-entered hounds. Hunts have the services of about 4,000 puppy walkers. There are 530 full-time employees and 360 part-time ones. Professional Masters bring the number to over 1,000 and there are about 30,000 Hunt subscribers and nearly 50,000 supporters' club members. An average of 300 Hunts hunt a total of 30,000 days each season. Attendance at meets by both mounted and foot followers exceeds 1,300,000.

I know statistics are boring, but the ones listed above illustrate how many families' livelihoods are dependent upon and affected by the sport. And these figures don't include the social element. Hunts organize over 4,000 social and equestrian functions, attended by nearly 1,500,000 people. The whole thing gives an indication of the scale of public involvement in hunting. Add to this the ancillary businesses which are, in varying degrees, dependent upon an income from hunting. They include feed merchants, saddlers, tailors, bootmakers, liveries and riding schools, farriers, country-clothing manufacturers, vets, suppliers of horse goods, hotels, pubs, farming and fencing contractors.

I rarely watch television, but on the few occasions when I have seen hunting televised, the traditional clothing worn out hunting is invariably perceived by those who don't hunt as offensive. The uniform of Hunt Servants and the etiquette of a correctly dressed field are seen as the hallmark of exclusivity and class distinction. Hunt Servants wear the livery of their profession, and being smartly turned out is an indication of the pride they take in their work and the service they provide to the farming community. A Master wears the same livery so that he is easily identifiable, and his standard of dress sets an example to the field. Hunting coats are practical; they are warm, waterproof and comfortable, which is why they have remained unchanged for several hundred years. Boots protect the leg; a stock protects the neck; breeches were specifically designed for riding. It is all a matter of common sense and the natural courtesy that field sports have encouraged for a thousand years. In the programme about hunting Clarissa and I were determined to show the opposite of the media portrayal of fox-hunting. There would be no lawn meets, no red coats. Not far from us was the ideal pack. They are kennelled in a farmyard and hunted, virtually single-handed, by the Master, Michael Hedley, who is also a hard-working tenant farmer.

This Hunt has provided a service, and a means of social communication across a huge area of remote upland Britain, for far longer than its date of registration in 1869. It is the main source of social contact amongst the isolated shepherds and hill farmers in its country. Once these joined the field on their hill ponies, as hounds hunted across their land. Many now ride quad-bikes. This was, particularly for us, an added bonus. Clarissa's riding days are temporarily in abeyance, but she would be able to follow on a quad-bike. We went down to see Michael and Carole Hedley at the end of November. Quick to see how the programme might help hunting and its role in the future of the countryside, Michael, with the open-handedness that is typical of him, readily agreed to do everything he could to help.

On the Tuesday after we got back from the Waterloo Cup, I travelled to Northumberland with Esmé to meet Michael and to have a look at the Border Hunt's country. It is fifty miles long and twenty-five miles wide, most of it hill and open moorland. A large part is in the Cheviots which is beautiful, blood-stirring country and dangerous ground to ride a quad-bike over. The meets during the week that had been scheduled for filming were all in the vicinity of the Cheviots.

The Border Hunt Foxhounds: 'They can kill anything but flying things, and even they have to be a good bit above the ground'

This presented a nightmarish logistical exercise for Esmé because, for the crew to follow hounds Esmé, Robin, Shu, Ed the new soundman, Steve, the gear and Clarissa were all to be mounted on quad-bikes.

At Hownam, where the hounds would meet, the Cheviots stand proud, majestic and very steep. The potential for disasters was endless. Nor was the matter improved by Michael's casual reference to frequent accidents and remarks that if hounds found a fox at this time of year, the chances were that it would be off like a scalded cat for the Otterburn Military Firing Ranges. As we drove back towards Edinburgh I could practically hear Esmé's brain churning as she grappled with the complexities of what lay ahead, and the consequences if something, in a programme fraught with political sensitivity, went wrong. To distract her I asked whether this sort of thing was different from the programmes she had worked on before.

'Different?' she cried wildly. 'Different? It's like being on the Planet Zog!'

At home there is a drawer full of cards and amongst them I found one with a photograph of a woman wearing scarlet lipstick and the inscription, 'The Red Badge of Courage'. Clarissa and I wrote in it 'Those who survive the Planet Zog can wear the Red Badge of Courage', and signed it 'The Zoggies'.

The week we spent with the Border was particularly magical. Michael and Carole Hedley are exceptional people, and the whole community gave generously in so many different ways and made us welcome. This is a close-knit fraternity bound together by the Hunt. Detectable amongst them was a puzzled anxiety. Why should an alien political party – which has cynically exploited the imbalance between the urban majority and the rural minority – wish to threaten their way of life?

Our first day's filming was at Michael's farm. Apart from his suckler cows and Cheviot ewes, Michael sells dog-meal. The story-line was that I should take Clarissa with me to collect a load. On the way there Clarissa complained that she had more interesting things to do than drive miles for a few sacks of dog food. I persuaded her that the journey would be worthwhile because there was going to be a SURPRISE.

We found Michael foot-rotting lambs, had the usual farmers' gripe about the weather, the Government and the continual slide in livestock prices, and discussed where the meet was that coming Saturday. We went to look at the sucklers and, as we rounded the corner of the cattle courts, came face to face with Clarissa's big surprise, a paddock full of foxhounds. These hounds are Michael's pride and joy. There are thirty couple of hill-hounds with whom he hunts three days a week. They average 100 days a season (from the beginning of November until the end of March) and kill around 200 foxes. The hounds are light and, as we discovered, very fast. They are bred on the lines of all hill-hounds, with a bit of Ullswater, College Valley and Dumfriesshire blood. These are the sort about whom Joe Dawson, the famous huntsman of the Patterdale hounds remarked, 'They can kill anything but flying things, and even they have to be a good bit above ground.' Michael does the hounds himself and, because collecting and skinning dead stock is out of the question, he feeds them a porridge made from the meal he sells. Hounds looked fit and healthy and I actually bought some of the dog-meal. My sheepdogs really did well on it at lambing.

Whilst Michael was discussing his hounds, three puppy walkers arrived to return puppies to the pack. Members of the Hunt have the opportunity to become very much involved in the career of individual hounds and Shirley, Fiona and Susan were respectively a district nurse and housewives, married to local farmers and shepherds. Between six or eight puppies are walked every year and these ladies always try to have one. It's a lovely thing to do, walking a hound pup, and it is an essential part of a young hound's upbringing. It gives them the chance to become acclimatized to farm life so they don't make fools of themselves on a hunting day. They can, also, be an absolute nightmare to look after, and one always swears never to have them again, but when you have walked a pup and it has been entered to the pack, its future career adds an extra interest to the fascination of watching hounds work.

It is a traumatic moment, returning a pup to kennels, not unlike leaving a child in the school playground for the first time. They are accepted with a surprising lack of fuss by the other hounds.

There is a fair amount of body talk and a few old hounds have a bit of a grumble for form's sake, but there is none of the resentment you might expect.

'They are ready to come back now. The hunting instinct is beginning to show and they will become difficult to handle soon,' Shirley said, talking to three hounds whom she had walked previously and who were standing on their hind legs greeting her through the paddock fence. A brood bitch had whelped recently and we were able to film the old lady lying proudly beneath a heater lamp with her nuzzling litter while Susan chose a pup that she would walk once it had

Puppy walkers with their charges

been weaned. To expand on the puppy-walking theme, that afternoon we filmed Craig Weir, the shepherd at the farm where we were to meet the following day. He was hunting his Cheviot ewes out of the valley bottoms to start their evening rake to high ground with three sheepdogs, a Lakeland terrier and, lolloping along behind his motor-bike, a hound puppy. Later on his wife took the hound puppy into their cottage to feed it.

That night in the Percy Arms I laid out my hunting kit. Over the last twenty-five years most of mine had either been lent to people or simply lost. All that remained were my boots, made by Tom Hill in 1968. The trees hadn't been out of them since they

went in after a day's hind hunting in 1975. Assiduous searching among trunks in the attic had produced an old black hunting coat made in 1923, and a pair of breeches, much chewed about by moths. Mr Lowe of Stewart Christie, the Edinburgh tailors, had worked wonders on the coat and stretched the boots to their limit. He also showed me a trick. If your boots are too tight, put plastic shopping bags on your feet. It beats talcum powder and helps keep your feet warm. Gradually I assembled stocks and boot-pulls, garter-straps, a stock-pin, a hunting shirt and I found my father's old waistcoat with the silver Trinity Foot Beagles' buttons. At enormous expense I purchased a hard hat, but the question remained: would this collection of virtually antique clothing hold together?

That particular anxiety paled into insignificance as I considered the awful potential for calamity

on the following day. I had not expected the BBC to attempt to film hounds hunting, simply because there is no telling which line a fox may decide to take, and attempting to keep hounds within filmable range would be virtually impossible. This is why most footage tends to be limited to meets. Neither did I expect them to film Clarissa and me participating as part of the field, on ground remotely as inaccessible to cameras as the Cheviots. The purpose of the programme, after all, was to illustrate how important hunting is in rural communities. A token involvement would have been adequate. Steve, however, was adamant that it should be part of the programme.

Clarissa is incredibly brave and, with alarming disregard for her own personal safety, game for anything. She has always been like this and this quality has remained unaffected by age, fame or infirmity. It was now exactly twelve weeks since her operation. With all of ten minutes' tuition on a quad-bike, she was blithely intending to ride one over country that even I, with ten years' experience, would have baulked at. When I suggested that this might not be prudent she boomed: 'I'm not missing a day's hunting and that's the end of it.'

Robin is the sort of chap who would cope with any situation. Steve and Ed were wildly enthusiastic but I doubted whether either of them had ever been on anything like a quad-bike before in their lives. Esmé and Shu had wisely decided to follow in a Land Rover and would, presumably, be able to get stunningly artistic shots of the helicopters coming across the Tweed Valley to take the survivors out on stretchers.

Earlier on, and wiping the tears from our eyes, Clarissa and I had thought up a side-splitting

ABOVE: With our hirelings
LEFT: Demonstrating the versatility of a boot hook

vignette for our arrival at the meet, with a build-up leading into it, which was intended to create the impression that she would be mounted. There had been a number of shots of her looking wistfully at various equines, including a Clydesdale, and dialogue with references to riding. We drove up in the Land Rover, towing a horse float. Clarissa went in through the side door and made horse-soothing noises, including such endearments as 'Get off my foot, damn you.' I lowered the tailgate and went into the horse float. Our intention was that Clarissa would then erupt out of the float riding a quad-bike with me clinging on behind her – absolutely brilliant, except that the quad-bike wouldn't start!

At the meet everything was hurry and bustle. Land Rovers, horseboxes and quad-bikes were arriving, people were unloading and getting mounted. Michael unboxed the hounds and Dickie Jeffries, from whom we were hiring a hunter for me, drew up with a lorry full of hirelings. With a plea to the Almighty that my coat would hold together, I scrambled aboard my hireling, a sensible-looking thoroughbred-cross called Denny, with the aid of the lorry tailgate. I was talking to a group of sporting Americans, who come over every year to spend a month with the Border after hunting finishes in Georgia, when Esmé ran up. Robin had managed to start Clarissa's quad-bike. The cameras were all set up and ready.

Clarissa and I were to move off together, side-by-side, discussing fox-hunting and its efficacy

Wrong fox!

as a means of vermin control. This was a scene to which considerable importance had been attached. But Michael doesn't hang about. He called hounds together, said 'Right then', and the field moved off. Despite my efforts, Denny moved off. I had tried to explain to the crew that hirelings tend to go with the flow, but it had fallen on deaf ears. I didn't see Clarissa and the crew, except in the distance, for another two hours.

Michael's first draw was a covert up the side of a steep slope above Heatherhope Burn. This was a blank, and he cast hounds off on the hillside further up where there was a big patch of dead bracken. Hounds soon put up a fox and were off, running up well together round the shoulder of the hill and out of view. Events happened very quickly thereafter. Michael's reputation for hard and fast riding, and his knowledge of the hills and hunting hill-hounds is as legendary as that of his predecessor, Jake Robson, who hunted these hounds for fifty-odd years from 1879 to 1933.

Hunting in the Cheviots is an art form of its own. The country is nearly all white hill, in places running up to 2,000 feet. It is a mixture of granite shale, peat, tussock grass and large stretches of damp moorland criss-crossed with drains and bog. Aficionados refer to hunting in the Cheviots as hill topping and there is no doubt that some of it is wonderful galloping country and unsurpassable for seeing. There is something thrilling beyond words about hounds appearing briefly on the lips of a succession of skylines – 'It's like hunting within arm's reach of heaven,' one of the Americans said. The field was nearly all shepherds and hill farmers who knew the ground as well as I know the hills at home. Even the Americans have hunted here often enough to know what they were doing. I, on the other hand, did not, and this part of the Cheviots is a network of deep, remote, steep-sided valleys, sickeningly steep as far as I was concerned. Hill topping is not for the faint-hearted and, gripped with periodic bouts of vertigo, I ignored Dickie Jeffries's advice to 'Shorten your stirrups and ride him on a loose rein. The old hoss knows where he's going.'

That was as may be. Even horses have their off days and I proceeded with extreme caution. The field, never very big in the first place, dwindled away to a handful, as those in the know took their own line.

The possibility of being lost in the middle of thousands of acres of hill and bog began to concern me and I attached myself to a sporting-looking cove called George, on a sturdy cob. He, I had noticed, had a walkie-talkie set clipped to his hunting coat. Obviously he was an official of some sort who would know the lie of the land. With growing confidence, I cantered along with him. It was one of those glorious days that were part of the false spring of early March 2000. Skylarks sang and the view across the Tweed Valley to the Lammermuirs was stunning – the reverse of the one I have seen so often from my highest ground.

Every now and again we would stop and listen. We could hear brief and blood-stirring snatches

I'm separated from Clarissa. I've lost my pipe, my Mars Bar and most of the skin off my arse, but I'm having a lovely time

of hounds speaking, borne back to us on the wind. Periodically, George's walkie-talkie would crackle and I asked him what role he had in the Hunt.

'None really,' he replied. 'We all help Michael where we can. If you know the country well, he gives you a radio.'

I asked him if he farmed round here.

'Good lord, no,' he replied. 'I'm a policeman.'

One of the most disconcerting things about hunting on the Cheviot is the way people suddenly disappear. Up on the tops, the immediate skyline is so small that the least break in concentration can leave you in sole possession of a magnificent view. This is what happened to me when I was trying to light my pipe. At one moment, I was part of a field of three, and striking matches inside my coat. When I emerged, puffing triumphantly, I was all alone. Following a fence, I eventually came to a gate tied with many strands of binder-twine. To the left of it was a length of post and railing. This was a rarity: it was one of the Borders, famous Hunt jumps and presented me with a quandary. Should I jump it, or get off and wrestle with the string? Both activities ran the risk of placing the final burden on the ancient stitching of my clothing, and there was always the possibility that I might topple out of the saddle. After some thought I decided to jump, but my heart wasn't in it and neither was Denny's. We were clearly lost and he too longed for home and a hot bath. We came to a gradual halt and at that moment Esmé and Shu materialized out of nowhere.

'I'll undo the gate for you,' Esmé offered.

Thirty years ago, in similar circumstances, a girl with blonde hair and blue eyes had appeared unexpectedly, offering to undo a gate. Then, as now, my manly pride was stung.

'Quite unnecessary,' I announced archly. 'There is a perfectly good jump.'

We were magnificent, Denny and I. A short run up and we were airborne. Shu's camera whizzed. There were girlish gasps of admiration. The ghost of Colonel Crawford – my old riding master at the Porlock Vale School of Equitation – pursed his lips with approval and, as we landed with cat-like agility and grace, I saw a small group of horsemen appear round the shoulder of the hill. These were the sporting Americans and we hurried forward together. Denny and I were no longer lost and, in the distance, I could hear the lovely music of Michael's hounds. From the sound of things there were great doings in the next valley. Riding over the crest of a ridge, we saw before us the rest of the field, both mounted and motorized, with, thankfully, Clarissa and the rest of the crew. Robin was bending over his camera and, on the steep face of the opposite hill, a fox was picking his way through a vast area of shale. Over the skyline came the hounds, owned the line through the shale and disappeared into the valley bottom. We could hear them in full cry somewhere below us, and then the final successful clamour.

That night after dinner in the Percy Arms, Clarissa, Steve and I joined Michael, still in his hunting kit, for a drink in the bar. It was packed with people who had been out that day and the craik was full of admiration for the crew and Clarissa's bravery. No one could believe that none of them had been on quad-bikes before, let alone kept up with hardened followers unscathed. The BBC were the heroes of the hour and Clarissa was a heroine bordering on the stature of a saint. It is a great area for singing and, at some later date, I could see a ballad of her deeds being added to their repertoire, to be sung on the anniversary of the occasion.

The atmosphere was euphoric and the ever-expanding party was all set to make a night of it when Steve, indicating it was time for their nightly contest, jerked his fist up and down.

'Coming, dear,' said Clarissa. She downed her lemonade and, bidding the company goodnight, meekly followed him through the bar. An awed silence fell. They had seen everything now.

D'ye ken John Peel's missus?

'Backgammon,' I said frantically. 'Every night they play backgammon.' Backgammon? They had never heard it called that before.

C The benign deity who had been with us throughout had definitely supplied Steve. When I first met him, I had found him urban, unknowledgeable and cold and had only Bob's reassurances to go on. Johnny actually went so far as to pronounce that asking 'that man to make a film on the countryside is like asking a deaf man to make a film about Mozart'. Fortunately, Steve is one of those happy men who has a totally open mind, a willingness to listen and quick grasp to learn. He has become not only a dear friend but has come to love and understand the country and its ways – his magic touch gilds our television efforts so beautifully. Sometimes it is nice to be wrong!

It is strange how often, in sobriety and middle age, I relive my life. I didn't sleep well that night in the Percy Arms due to an emotion I am not much prone to: fear. To be brutally honest I was scared something rotten. It had seemed a huge joke not to tell the BBC that the only experience I had had driving a quad-bike before was ten minutes or so on Johnny's hill when his fifteen-year-old son had taught me to ride it. He had inherited his father's – and his grandfather's – ability to pass on knowledge clearly. I just hoped he had done his job properly. My mind flew back forty years to another such occasion when I was about to set out on my first hunting expedition. This time it was tweed breeches and cashmere socks which I'd donned like a matador putting on his suit of lights, and wondering in what state he would return from the fight. Then it was the tight-fitting jodhpurs and well-cut hacking jacket of childhood. But this time the joke had gone cold on me. I knew the country we would be hunting over: its huge hills plunge remorselessly into heart-stopping gullies that had claimed lives and cracked skulls only that year. A young shepherd we had met earlier, still bears the scar which had nearly taken his life when he couped his bike and was helicoptered to Newcastle Infirmary. Strangely, on both this occasion and the one that had so vividly returned from my childhood, my fear was not that I should be killed, but that I would be proved inadequate and make a fool of myself. I defocused, as is my wont, by worrying about Johnny and I managed to work myself into quite a lather over his well-being on a strange horse. I remembered reading about Alexander and Bucephalus – his famous charger – and their exploits. It comforted me when I remembered that Alexander too had red hair – bizarre, the human brain.

Johnny and I took the Land Rover to the meet and gassed away as usual. The only signs of our mutual concern were remarks such as, 'Remember, Clarissa, never take your thumb off the throttle whilst going uphill.' (Throttle? I panicked.) Or 'Johnny, dear, don't forget to check your girth regularly with all those hills.' This was greeted with a dismissive 'Pshaw', but the giveaway was that these words were inserted, seemingly irrelevantly, into conversations about something quite else.

When there was no sign of Dickie Jeffries at the meet, Esmé went pale. We decided to film the scene where I drove the quad-bike out of the horsebox. I mounted the quad-bike, Johnny dropped the flap, I gunned the starter and nothing happened. The bike would not start. Scores of lovely young men sprang to my aid and, after much talk of valves, blockages and other male-bonding things, it still wouldn't start. It was then that we discovered Steve had turned off the fuel tank. Dickie Jeffries arrived eventually and Johnny mounted. Esmé announced: 'Panic officially over.'

At the puppy return I had met Shirley, the district nurse. She was to lead me, and I greeted her gratefully.

Michael Hedley, resplendent in a yellow roadman's jacket over his hunting gear, greeted us and for the first time in years I raised my forefinger to my cap to say 'Morning, Master.' The only problem is that crash helmets don't have brims. Hounds were unloaded and sniffed about, cocking the odd leg and being bawled at; people mounted and swore at their horses, greeted each other cheerfully, and swigged the odd stirrup-cup out of plastic mugs. There was that wonderful smell of leather, warm horse, fresh dung and the strange tangy odour of hound. I sat on my squat little quad-bike and felt unbelievably happy and excited. Johnny was getting the feel of his horse and grinned at me and the years rolled back. We could have been fifteen again and getting ready for just such a day under a Sussex sky, with the rolling line of the Downs before us.

Esmé had asked Johnny and me to move off side-by-side so that she could film us together. The only trouble was that Johnny's horse hated quad-bikes, as we soon found out when I drove up alongside. The last I saw of him he was travelling fast sideways, with that strange cross-legged gait that denotes a horse fighting for control. Johnny was swearing happily and enjoying the contest. I didn't see them again until the first stand when they had clearly bonded and Johnny looked as insouciant as he usually does on a horse.

I don't know if you have ever ridden a quad-bike – they are a great invention and perfect for whizzing about over steep hills – but I don't advise that you spend your first real time on one following a fast hunt over really daunting hills. As I shot up the first incline, remembering to

Moving off

keep my thumb firmly on the throttle, I looked back to see Steve, who had been hired a quad-bike with virtually bald tires, standing still as the wheels went round and round! How he managed to keep up at all was a mystery. Robin and Ed the soundman were whizzing about having a lovely time and so, once I got my confidence, was I. There was a heady moment when, as hounds took, off I saw a dashing young man shoot over the brow of the hill, obviously knowing where he was going. I followed his lead and – wheee! – a one-in-three drop. Well, if he could do it, so could I and, remembering my tutor's imprecations to let the quad-bike pick its way downhill on the engine without using the throttle, I made my way down this monstrous abyss. Fortune favours the brave and I reached the bottom in time to see the fox weaving its way through the gorse and scree on the opposite side, with hounds following its line with grim determination. There, in front of Robin's camera, was a classic pursuit and kill, with the lead hound dispatching the fox with a quick bite to the back of the neck – you know, the way the antis deny that it happens.

I sat there feeling very smug. I was yards from the kill and receiving, from a Heathcliff of a Northumbrian on a big bay horse, the accolade that I was 'sum rider'. Despite the presence of Robin, I had so much forgotten I was filming that I was quite short with Esmé when she arrived and requested me to talk to the assembled followers for camera! We found a fresh scent and chased up hill and dale before it was time to leave. I met up with Johnny intermittently and we beamed fondly at each other, euphoric about the amazing country, the camaraderie of the Hunt and the fact that we had acquitted ourselves so well. Afterwards I had a bath: the best bath in all the world is the one that follows a day's hunting.

Due to the vagaries of a faulty tape we hadn't been able to film some of our first day's hunting and so we were lucky enough to have a second day out with the Border. That day was incredibly sunny and rather different from the snow showers that fell on our first outing. At one stop everyone was off their horses and lying around on the grass sunbathing! Robin was as determined to get a fox as any huntsman and, despite the hot weather, Michael killed three that day. Johnny, by now bonded with Denny, was still unable to persuade him to tolerate quad-bikes. This second day's hunting was a joint meet with the Ullswater, who are a Cumbrian fell pack. Because it was a joint meet, and because it was the last day of the season, there was a large field and more quad-

In Dickie Jeffries' stables

bikes than usual. I saw Ed, the soundman, at the top of the hill and asked where Johnny was. Ed, who could hear Johnny on his radio-mike, listened for a moment and replied, 'Spending quality time with his horse, I think.' Whatever Johnny said to Denny it must have worked, because we were able to film the last shot of us riding home side-by-side, like a latter day Don Quixote and Sancho Panza, talking of the day's events and our resolve to fight to educate those who don't understand why hunting is such a necessary part of life in the countryside. It is estimated that the loss to the economy of the Scottish Borders alone – which supports seven packs and two cross-Border packs – would be between £3.5m and £4m per annum, and 300 jobs would be lost if hunting is banned. This would be dreadful for the Borders, which are in economic recession as it is.

One of the many jobs that depends upon the Hunt for its existence is that of the liverymen. Denny, Johnny's hireling for the two days, came from a livery stable owned by Dickie Jeffries in Northumbria. Dicky has about thirty horses in livery and hires them out to people to hunt during the season. His stable has easy access to about five Hunts, of which the Border is one. It is customary, where possible, for the hirer to visit the liveryman and discuss his capabilities and try out a horse for suitability. This Johnny had been unable to do because of our tight filming schedules, but we filmed it after the event, for the programme.

Dicky is a hunting farmer who, when the rural economy went into free-fall, converted his barns into stables and filled them with horses for hire. Keeping a livery is incredibly hard work, but it is a wonderful way for those who want to be around horses to make a living. Apart from the hirelings, people who have perhaps not got the money, or the property, the inclination or the time to look after horses on a daily basis board them with a good liveryman at a fixed rate. This is an important part of the horse economy and provides income for a great many people. Dickie told me that he would have to let at least two of the girl grooms – who are in full-time employment – go if hunting is banned. Apart from stabling, and some riding-camp work in the summer, the liveryman's main income comes from hunting.

When we arrived to film at Dickie's stables, there was a young smith, with a travelling smithy, shoeing outside the stables. Johnny and I were surprised that no one on the production team paid any attention to him. We pointed out his presence to Steve and we filmed an interview with the smith, a fine, burly young man, who said that more than 30% of all his work comes from the Hunt, and that he had two full-time apprentices, but would have to lay off one and reduce the other to half-time, if hunting was banned.

We then interviewed Dickie and, if Mr Blair wants further proof that hunting should not be banned, he should have been there. Dickie, who is a retiring almost diffident type with a slight stutter and a slouch because of his height, does not seem to be the sort of man to manifest aggression but rather tolerance and a gentle sense of humour. But when I asked him how he felt about the proposed ban on hunting, he suddenly became transformed, standing straight as an arrow, so you could tell that his wiry frame was all muscle. His jaw set like a Victorian hero's and, without a trace of his stutter, he made it very clear that he would not suffer uninformed urban interference. Dickie said, 'I am tired of those people in towns who know nothing about the countryside, and can't even keep their own environment safe, telling us what to do. Now they are trying to pass laws based on their ignorance. We won't stand for it and they must take the consequences if they continue.'

I was left in no doubt that he would fight to keep his source of income, and his ability to provide employment for local people. It was heart-warming, stirring stuff and the change in the way he stood when he spoke out against urban interference surprised Robin and Esmé quite a bit, I think.

The smell and sounds of the livery stables were very evocative to me, as were the horse that put its ears back and bit, the curious one that nuzzled for treats and a fat, hairy, bay pony just like my Aster. When I was a child, my sister Heather kept her show working hunter with the great Dick Stillwell, who helped her with schooling, and boxed him, and my mother's hunter, to meets. His stables were just outside Windsor with easy access to the heady hunting of the Oxfordshire Downs, as well as the smaller Berkshire pastureland. Endless hours were spent posting to the trot along the hedgerows – which my sister called 'hedgehopping' – before taking off across the gentle fields. The equine world of a London child is most usually the world of the livery stable. If hunting is successfully banned, those urban children will lose the chance to experience the countryside in the way that they have come to love, and the liverymen will lose one of their chief sources of income.

The Hunt is exceedingly important socially too. We filmed the post-Hunt ceilidh, which was held in the village hall. Johnny, who dances beautifully, but has an abhorrence of doing such things among strangers (never mind the millions of viewers out there!) had been mobbing Esmé up to give him dancing lessons. Esmé had danced Scottish dancing competitively and has that wonderful stance that goes with the art, but he got short shrift from her. Tra la. We were both filmed dancing, then Michael and I stumbled through a Scottish waltz, and Johnny and Carole, Michael's wife, spun like teetotums in the Gay Gordons. Shu asked Johnny to dance, Esmé was shamed into making up the set and Robin filmed it all with glee. Never has my hero leapt so high, and so lightly, at the eightsome reel which seemed to go on forever. Only I, happily sucking a lemonade on the side lines, could tell from long practice that he was absolutely knackered, but not prepared to show it or give in!

On a more serious note, now that many churches no longer organize social occasions, all that is left in many country areas is the Hunt. Farming is a lonely life and at the end of a long and tiring day, the thought of setting to and entertaining are fairly daunting. There is little for the young communally, and nowhere for them to meet. The Hunt organizes endless gatherings from formal Hunt Balls, so beloved of the media, to the more usual dances, barbecues, suppers and singing evenings. Singing is very popular and the joint meet of our second day was followed by a very enthusiastic singing contest which we sadly had to miss. The ceilidh we attended raised £4,000 for the Leukaemia Unit at the Newcastle Infirmary as a thank-you for their care of a Hunt member.

The combination of the cross-section of ages, the sense of community and the shared interest have given me more fun at such gatherings than at parties costing many thousands of pounds.

Joe Smith digs in

As we left the ceilidh the Commandant of the Otterburn Ranges remarked, 'If hunting went, there would be no village hops and all the old traditional dances would be lost.'

The sense of community, and the feeling of well-being that belonging to a like-minded group brings with it, would also be lost. There is an acknowledged statistic that rural suicides are 30% lower in areas where there is a strong Hunt. If hunting is banned, the loss of this sense of belonging will have a devastating effect on many rural communities, so will the consequent losses to their local economies, not to mention the losses of the animals upon which they depend, as they fall prey to roaming foxes.

Our production team had become so fascinated by all these aspects of the Hunt that it was difficult to lure them away. But we managed to persuade them to film sea-coaling at Ashington.

I knew nothing about sea-coaling until we went to Ashington, but I had read all the literary allusions to 'The devil sitting by his good sea coals' in Shakespeare and endless references in Dickens and Trollope. But I think I imagined it was like the monks at Whitekirk who took the coal from the sea where a seam had opened into the water. It was Johnny who knew about Ashington from twenty-odd years ago when he was a mud student. His wife, Mary, had given birth to their daughter there.

Lest you doubt me when I tell you that Johnny is inseparable from his terrier of the day, you should know that he went into the birthing room with Trooper, his Jack Russell, under his coat. A good terrier will keep perfectly still and quiet in that position, and such is Johnny's irresistible charm that the nurses let both of them stay. I asked Mary what she thought about this. She said that as the nurses had spent all day looking for the source of a terrible smell – it was the packet of 'fresh' prawns he had put, as a treat, in her bedside locker – the terrier was as nothing.

It was in his wanderings round Ashington during this period that Johnny came across the sea-coalers. These hardy souls, many of whom are gypsies, inhabit a strange world along the coast where the wild rugged Northumbrian scenery gives way to the colliery and power station. The piebald and skewbald horses that pull the coaling carts, and the little gypsy racing carts, gallop

Going sea-coaling

about amid this strange landscape, and the sea is grey, even on the brightest day, because it is full of coal dust.

The colliery, the last in the area, washes its coal in the sea and the smaller coals fall through the machinery and remain in the sea. This waste coal is washed up into the shallows and turns the beach black. The sea-coalers back their carts into the sea and, with the use of a large metal net scoop known as the 'chip-pan', they transfer the coal to their carts, allowing the waves to wash away the excess sand. They also 'skim' the waste coal from the top of the sand with a shovel. This is hard and heavy work, but a fit sea-coaler can collect a great deal of coal this way. We went to see Joe Smith, one of the last of the old-timers, who lives in a caravan by the beach. He is a fit and youthful-looking sixty-seven-year-old, and is looked after by his three sisters, who take it turn to do his washing and provide for him. His oldest sister can remember how the family got into sea-coaling when their father, a miner, won the Football Pools, got drunk, went to Newcastle and came back with a horse. It was winter and snowing, so he brought the horse into the kitchen and they all came down the next morning and found it there. Their father used to sea-coal to supplement his income.

Joe took us out with him and we were amazed to see that he simply piles up his coal and puts a stone, with his initials on it, on top of the pile. He leaves the coal for the haulier to collect, weigh and then pay him for it. Ironically, because sea-coals are small and burn very slowly – due to the amount of seawater in them – they are mostly sold to the power station. There is a small domestic market, but this largely went during the miners' strikes when sea-coalers were accused of being blacklegs, despite the fact that if the colliery wasn't working there could be no coal for them to collect. The colliery at Ashington may close soon and then there will be two years' worth of coal to wash, and that will be an end of sea-coaling in Ashington. I asked Joe about the Shakespearean quote and he said the earliest sea-coalers made their living from coal spillages from barges. Joe got into sea-coaling because he had a weak chest, and couldn't endure the coal dust in the pit. He was a weakly boy and it was thought unlikely that he would survive long. But hard work and sea air have made him hale and healthy, yet this is not a job that is likely to be protected by anyone.

It rather looked as if we were going to be stranded in Ashington when the Land Rover refused to start. This was particulary irritating as it was beginning to get dark and extemely cold. Robin and Johnny spent an age peering into the engine. Then Steve gave the ignition key a turn, as people do when they are trying to be helpful, and the damn thing hiccuped into life!

CHAPTER SIX

A RAM'S HORN AND A RUBBER GLOVE

J The obvious choice of venue was on the hill land that I farm in southern Scotland. I had mixed feelings about this. For one thing I would be flat out with my lambing, but there were other concerns. I had been anxious at the prospect of taking the BBC into the lives of other people and the boot was now on the other foot. I agonized briefly about whether the aspects of hill farming that mean so much to me would ever be captured on camera: the exquisite joy when winter's long silence is broken by the song of migratory birds coming to nest on the moorland in spring; the first lambs of a new lambing which never cease to fascinate me, particularly as I can trace their breeding back to rams I bought years ago; my respect for the hardy little hill ewes, my love for the sheepdogs and the sheer antiquity of the land; the freedom of the broad horizon; the triumphs and disasters of another lambing.

After four months of intensive working conditions we had begun to respect the crew as highly trained professionals and to like them as people. Their eyes had been opened to a world that was completely alien to them. They had been charmed by the courtesy of our contributors. Without compromising their personal views they were developing an understanding and sensitivity towards the countryside and the importance of our rural way of life. We were proceeding on a basis of mutual trust and I was confident that Esmé, Steve and Chloë would do their best. In any case, sharing the experience with Clarissa was bound to be a hoot.

I have run my farming operations single-handedly, with part-time staff at lambing and shearing. My family has always been involved and, with the help of long-suffering dogs, we somehow manage to cope with sheep numbers that once provided employment for four shepherds. Hill farming has remained virtually unchanged for 300 years, except for advances in veterinary science and the invention of the all-terrain vehicle, or quad-bike, which has done away with the traditional hill pony and indeed many shepherds. However, when the programmes were commissioned, a full-time shepherd was obviously going to be needed to take my place. I was tremendously lucky to hear of a young New Zealander who was prepared to take the job on for a year. New Zealand is a nation of stockmen and an extremely civilized place. It has twenty-nine harrier packs, stalking, pig-hunting, shooting and some of the finest fishing in the world. It is a country for which I have a deep affection – a married daughter lives there and I regret that it is so far away. New Zealand's remoteness has been the country's saving grace, because it is still underpopulated and the people retain a set of values, courtesy and charm which have been eroded in other countries.

Tony Gallen, a farmer's son from near Wanganui, has become a family friend and he made it possible for me to accommodate an increasing workload. He seemed to regard his responsibility as a challenge: and his mission in life to relieve me of the stress of day-to-day farming while we filmed the programmes. Also, as a countryman, he appreciated why the programmes were being made.

They were canny men, the early graziers. Heather is a surprisingly fragile plant, easily damaged by overgrazing. So, to preserve the delicate ecological balance, each area of hill was assessed for stocking rate and then only the safe number of ewes were taught to live on those particular areas. These were known as hefts, and the initial process of hefting was enormously time-consuming. Circular stone walls called stells were built near each heft and the sheep were shut in them at night. By day, a boy or an old man stayed with them to see that they did not stray from their allocated hefts. Because they are practically wild animals, hill sheep are very territorial and these new flocks gradually became acclimatized to their own ground. To maintain this, all the five-year-old ewes were sold off the hefts annually, and an equivalent number of ewe lambs retained, thus grazing territories became inherited knowledge. Eventually the sheep were no longer shut in at night, but instinctively made for the security and safety of high ground in the evenings. During the day they grazed downhill to the better grazing in the valley bottoms. To ensure an even grazing pattern, shepherds encouraged their sheep to keep on the move, pushing them downhill in the mornings and up again at night. They still do this today.

How do we get out again?

To me, the beauty of hill farming is working with animals in their natural environment and that which they share with many species of wildlife, rarely seen elsewhere. In all other forms of stock husbandry, animals have had to adjust to man's environment and much of their survival instinct has disappeared. To farm the vast unfenced areas of moorland you have to utilize the sheep's natural behavioural pattern. You must know the ground they live on like the back of your hand, the plant life that grows there and their places of refuge in times of illness and bad weather.

Dante's inferno

None of it would be possible without sheepdogs. In 1800 James Hogg, the Ettrick Shepherd, wrote: 'Without the shepherd's collie, the Highlands of Scotland would not be worth a sixpence.'

Heather burning to create regeneration is as old as farming, but until the Agricultural Revolution, at the start of the eighteenth century, it was only carried out in a small way. The heather moorland that we know today as an attractive feature of Northern England and Scotland was painstakingly reclaimed from untamed heath by graziers as they established their flocks.

Using a system of rotational burning, and a carefully controlled stocking rate, these early flock-masters discovered that in the place of scrub, thistles, old rank heather and vigorously growing weed, an even spread of heather could be maintained. With the development of the shotgun and, in particular, the invention of the breech-loader in 1850, there was a massive increase in shooting and the demand for shooting tenancies. Sportsmen began to notice that moors managed by graziers carried more grouse than those that weren't. It was the start of a successful partnership between sheep and grouse, with heather burning playing a vital role in moorland management for both. If heather is not burnt, the plants become old and stemmy and lack nutritional value for either sheep or grouse. A properly managed moor has a mosaic pattern of different ages and lengths of heather, which are burnt rotationally to provide continual regrowth. This ensures that sheep graze evenly, and grouse and other ground-nesting moorland birds, many of whom are refugees from lowland monoculture, have the depth of cover they require to nest in safety from aerial predators. It also provides them with a space for their chicks to learn to fly, and a supply of essential plant food. Young heather shoots are the main food source for both sheep and grouse.

Muirburn is strictly governed by legislation. Below 1,500 feet it is only legal between 1 October and 15 April. There is an extension of fifteen days for ground above that altitude and, in both cases, if it is particularly wet, an extension of fifteen days may be granted. Although in practice there are six months in which to burn heather, most of it takes place from mid-March. The most important factor is to stop burning before the ground-nesting birds have laid their eggs. Heather burning has become quite high-tech since the days when I first started, when it could be very fraught indeed. The aim was to burn areas thirty yards wide and about twice as long. The face of a fire can broaden incredibly quickly and it took as many able-bodied men, thrashing with long-handled shovels, as one could bribe with promises of unlimited beer, to keep the thing under control. A runaway fire is a terrifying experience and can do incalculable damage to a valuable grouse moor. People still talk of one that got away near here. It burned thousands of acres of heather and kept the people of Edinburgh, thirty miles away, entertained by lighting up the night sky.

But it seemed that we were never going to get the right weather. It had been so wet that virtually no one in the area had managed to burn anything like the hoped-for acreage. Time was slipping by and the last possible filming date was the end of the week: after that it would be illegal to burn. It was Mull all over again, with endless telephone calls to the Meteorological Office and to the keepers. At the eleventh hour, when conditions were anything but suitable for burning, Jim Houliston, the keeper, agreed to burn some old long heather that needed taking out. As the crew were assembling the gear I could see black rain clouds moving up towards us from the coast. It was snow by the time it reached us, and the whole hill was dusted white.

'That's torn it,' I thought, 'Our luck's finally run out.'

Fire control

Down at the lambing shed I met Jim loading the shovels, heather torches and face masks into the Land Rover.

'Not burning, surely?' I asked.

'Hard to believe,' he said, 'but that snow shower completely missed the bit we want to burn.'

Absolutely incredible. We hurried out on to the hill where Jim had selected some old rough heather. He dribbled a thirty-yard line of diesel through the heather, lit it with the heather torch and we were away. Ever seeking the rib-tickle, the BBC had come up with the idea of Clarissa appearing in the middle of the moor with a fire extinguisher. Once we had got that out of the way, Clarissa was filmed discussing the purpose and importance of heather burning with Jim, whilst I flailed enthusiastically with a long-handled shovel. Once again the air was full of that sweet smell of burnt honey synonymous with approaching spring and the arrival of our migratory birdlife. However, the Land Rover managed to ruin our sense of achievement. It was feeling particularly evil-tempered that day and our combined efforts to coax it back into life were all to no avail. It had to be rescued by a tractor.

When we filmed the lambing Clarissa sat, like an empress, on a bale of straw in the quad trailer as I did my morning rounds. We talked about how, at lambing time, hill shepherds utilize the sheep's habit of grazing downhill in the mornings and back to the tops in the afternoons. Sheep hanging back at either time have recently lambed, are about to, or have a problem. For one section of filming we were alone except for the Sony Handycam mounted on the trailer. On top of my highest ground, where a set of whales' jawbones had once been erected, Clarissa announced that her morning coffee needed jettisoning. I stopped and let her out of the trailer and, with no cover about, was instructed to make myself scarce.

'Don't want anyone to see me,' she muttered, peering about cautiously and settling down behind the trailer. We'd forgotten about the camera and the delicate moment is now in the BBC archives, recorded for posterity.

We filmed larsen traps and rabbit boxes. Spring is the time of plenty for carrion crows, one of the most voracious moorland predators. There is a plentiful supply of ground-nesting birds' eggs and, as their own chicks hatch, the chicks of others, particularly grouse, form part of their diet. There are weakly lambs to blind and eat at leisure as they die. We put out larsen traps to catch them in the spring. A larsen trap is a cage with two compartments. In one side there is a lure bird that is fed and watered daily; some eggs bait the other side. An inquisitive crow will land on the perch which supports a hinged lid on the baited side. The perch collapses and the lid shuts. Larsen traps have to be checked every day and the trapped crow is destroyed far more humanely than the way in which it destroys its victims.

We use rabbit boxes because, over the last decade, that disgusting invention of a French scientist, myxomatosis, has become less effective, with the result that in our part of the world, the rabbit population has exploded. Rabbits live on the moorland and graze into neighbouring arable fields. As their numbers increase, they move deeper and deeper into the moor, fouling the heather – which eventually destroys it – thus depriving the grouse and the sheep of their food.

Sup up, lad

Some rabbits live in the heather above ground, others in gigantic warrens which are too big to gas or ferret. To try to arrest the damage we run small-gauge wire mesh along the fences separating moorland from improved marginal land. Where there are rabbit runs, metal boxes are dug in under the mesh. These boxes have tilting lids with a metal tube running over the top of them. The lid is kept rigid until rabbits have become accustomed to the tunnels. Then the retaining pin is removed and rabbits going through the tunnels fall into the box. By law the boxes have to be checked daily and the contents humanely dispatched. The whole exercise is enormously expensive, particularly as there is no market for the rabbits.

Clarissa, blissfully in her element and largely ignoring the cameras, carried on in her role of an ovine Florence Nightingale, resplendent in knee breeches and tam-o'-shanter, injecting ewes

that had had a difficult lambing with penicillin, bottle-feeding lambs, cleaning out pens and putting down new bedding. There is a splendid scene where she presided over a relatively recent procedure for persuading a ewe to accept an orphan lamb. The ewe's dead lamb is put into a bucket of hot water with as much afterbirth as possible. The dead lamb is removed after the recommended interval and the orphan lamb is dunked in the soupy water. When the lamb is presented to the ewe it is steaming hot, smells like her own and, hopefully, she will believe it to be hers. There is a surreal shot of the world's most famous cook vigorously stirring the bucket with a large wooden spoon.

Most of the ewes lamb out on the hill, with a couple of hundred brought into in fields. These are ewes from the furthest away heft on the farm. Bringing them in to fields reduces the time it takes to go round that part of the hill. A job we do daily is to walk ewes and lambs out of the fields back on to the hill. The reward for doing this successfully is the sight of them splitting off in different directions towards their own hefts. Blackie ewes hate being in fields so this must feel like being released from prison. The job can be great fun, with a lot of fast quad-bike work and clever dogging. We separate ewes with lambs from those that have still to lamb. There were some magnificent shots of Clarissa hurtling about happily on the quad-bike wearing her tam-o'-shanter, Robin's German Army waterproof poncho and a pair of Gucci sunglasses.

One of the things we desperately wanted to film was a natural birth, but this had so far eluded us. Like the births of most wild animals, the birth of a lamb is carried out quickly and, as far as possible, in secret. It often happens just before daybreak. During a sequence when Clarissa was cooking bacon butties for Tony Gallen and Ben and Shelley – two more New Zealanders who

ABOVE: Clarissa's first lamb
LEFT: Paramedics arrive

had come for the lambing – my son rode in on his motor-bike to announce that he knew where there was a ewe lambing. Robin, Shu, Esmé and Steve were tied up with Clarissa and the New Zealanders, which left Chloë. Although she did a tremendous amount behind the scenes, on shooting days Chloë's role was to ensure that everything ran smoothly and that the coffee was up to celebrity standard. A ewe giving birth was her big opportunity. Steve thrust the Sony Handycam into her hands and we piled onto the quad-bike and took off up the hill.

Hill ewes are easily spooked and seem to be able to halt the birth process if disturbed. When we were within fifty yards, Chloë got off the quad-bike and, with infinite care, sneaked up on the ewe with the camera pinned to her eye. She squatted down about ten yards away and waited, camera whirring. I suspected, when I saw the ewe, that there was a problem. She was lying in the bottom of an old quarry, an unlikely choice for a ewe to lamb in. After a bit I went over, quickly caught the ewe and made my inspection. There was a problem all right, and of the worst sort. It was a breech birth, with the lamb stuck across the ewe's pelvis, dead and cooking. There is no smell like it this side of hell.

Poor little gimmer. With difficulty I eased the head out but the ewe's pelvis was too small to get my hand past it to find a leg. This is quite the foulest job at lambing time and must be horrific if you have never seen it before. To get the rotten lamb out, the head has to be cut off, for a start. Behind me I heard an anguished intake of breath. Chloë was sticking gamely to her camera – most people would have run a mile. It was one of those nightmare lambings where I gave a silent and fervent prayer of thanks that I had stuffed a plastic veterinary glove into my pocket. The lamb had to come out piecemeal and still Chloë filmed. Finally the job was done and, as I helped the ewe to her feet, there was a shriek from Chloë. I turned round to see her dancing backwards, hand clutched to her mouth.

'What the hell's the matter?' I asked.

'Oh God, that was awful. I've just trodden in something that squelched.'

We live right on the edge of hunting country and fox control falls to the keepers. Throughout the winter they are constantly setting and checking snares, lying out at dusk and daybreak, beating through the big block of plantation that forms part of the farm. After a fall of snow they go out searching for tracks. At lambing, foxes are particularly busy. Vixens have cubs by then, they take a lot of feeding, and the moor is full of nesting game. It is also the time that keepers can most effectively reduce fox numbers by killing vixens and cubs underground. If moorland predators, both wing and fur, were not controlled the ground-nesting bird population would gradually diminish as it already has in certain parts of the country. Without game-birds there would be no gamekeepers and the management of our scenic uplands would either become a burden to the taxpayer or cease altogether.

We always get a certain amount of fox bother despite the keepers' vigilance. Sometimes just the occasional lamb goes missing, to be found again as an odd leg chewed clean, amongst the litter scraped out of an earth. Two years ago a fox played merry hell in a field of ewes and twin lambs. Morning after morning, until it was shot, I would find a lamb with its head missing, or bitten through the neck. Worse, none of the ewes would mother up. A black-faced ewe with twin lambs, when faced with danger, will eventually abandon one of them.

On Easter Day Clarissa drove down a precipitous part of the farm on the quad-bike. Without turning a hair she roared up a three-in-one slope, turned the bike round and happily drove along the edge of a cliff. Halfway along she shouted, 'Oi, there's something in the bottom. Looks like a lamb.' Sure enough in the bottom of a deep narrow cleugh, half covered in gravel, was the partially eaten body of a lamb. The fox had marked it and there was the unmistakable stink of fox pee. There wasn't a ewe in sight. A hill ewe will stick with a lamb when it's dead under pretty well any circumstances, except when a fox or dog has killed it.

I telephoned Jim and told him about the lamb. As far as he knew, none of the earths on the farm were working. He went round them all that afternoon to check that a vixen hadn't moved a split litter in. Cubs would be growing now and the earths they were born in could be getting pretty foul and overcrowded. But there was no sign of any of the earths being cleaned out, so that night we tried fox lamping. Jim drove us round part of the hill that he would expect a fox to come in on. He took us to nearby woodland, and a section of a neighbour's land where a part-time keeper might have missed an unoccupied earth. I swept the powerful spot lamp slowly backwards and forwards across the hill while Jim described the difference between the steady reflection of sheeps' eyes in the glare of the lamp and the flickering ones of a fox. It was a lovely evening, a brilliant starlit night with the whole panorama of the streetlamps of the coastal towns twinkling on either side of the Firth. We saw sheep and lambs, hundreds of rabbits and occasionally a hen grouse would helicopter into the air in alarm. In the back of the Land Rover, Robin and Martin, the new soundman, cursed softly as they were bounced up and down.

We saw no fox, but our presence would have been enough to deter one travelling in. That

Nell the starlet

lamb was the only one we had lost and I heard, later in the week, that a neighbouring keeper had shot a fox near the march fence.

Johnny has been a hill farmer now for twenty-five years, so I have got over the shock that the boy I always saw in my mind's eye as deeply cool, rather glamorous and never off a horse should have chosen such a hard path. We were both born to money and privilege and had it removed: in my case by my own dissolute hand, in Johnny's by his father's unlucky investment. Whether I would have been a cook or he a hill farmer if things had been different I can't tell, but we would both have missed out on very rewarding parts of our respective lives if we hadn't.

Hill farming is frequently what Johnny describes as primitive and not very pretty. On a good day the scenery is wonderful and the sheep, especially with their lambs, look pretty and friendly. But it is grindingly hard work: all hours on the hill in snow, hail and driving rain, and not particularly fragrant. The smell of afterbirth drying on a coat in a heated Land Rover is not easily forgotten. I used to ponder long and hard about why Johnny had chosen this hill-farming career until I realized the truth. The hill sheep is not the stolid often stupid sheep of the valleys. It is an admirable creature, a good mother, a great survivor (you can guess whose brain washed mine on this), but above all it is the closest thing to a wild animal that we farm in the British Isles. Johnny's fundamental quality is that he is a wild creature too. He is not lacking in social graces and you can always find him at a party by the group of mesmérized, good-looking women; not uneducated (I reluctantly have to admit he is probably better read than I am), just wild in the sense that he has an untameable spirit that is happiest in the wildest places. I suppose this must therefore hold true of others of his kind: all those hill farmers who pit themselves, with their sheep, against the elements.

As a cook, one of the things that strikes me as really stupid is the way hill sheep are handled once they go to market. Here you have the most organic of meat, tasting of the heather and the wind with nothing to supplement its diet (except, perhaps, a few sugar beet pellets fed to a ewe in the lambing season). But it is taken off the hill to be fattened up on tasteless feed so that it will produce a carcass that satisfies a butcher's specifications and taste of nothing. We buy Angus beef and Scottish salmon as luxury goods, so why not Hill lamb? I know that David Lidgate of the Q Guild – a division of excellence within the butchery trade – is trying to persuade the Meat and Livestock Commission to add a new specification to recognize different breeds of lamb which reach different weights and sizes. However, in a world where Whitehall accidentally lopped ten months off the slaughter age of beef following the BSE scare, and then refused to admit their mistake and alter it, my hopes aren't high. Consumer pressure is the only thing that has any effect. I am the Patron of the Association of Farmers' Markets and I have high hopes that through them we can begin to introduce organically fed hill sheep to the market. If people are given the chance to taste the real thing then, hopefully, they will keep on wanting it.

My exposure to Johnny's lambing has always been as a voyeur. True, when we were children he dragged me through ditches and had me disembowelling and skinning rabbits, but that was at my insistence. In previous years I have gone up to the Lammermuirs and gone out on the hill with Johnny in the Land Rover. We have driven round endlessly looking for ewes in distress, raking sheep back up the hill and watching the dogs work. However, the times have been of my choosing and, due to the human condition and the feeling that perhaps I wasn't much help anyway, these occasions have mostly tended to be in good weather. I enjoyed the companionship, the spring birdsong, the beauty of the hills and Johnny waxing eloquent on nature, but I admitted to myself it was a treat for me, not a help to Johnny.

But Johnny is the most responsible of stockmen and is really only happy if he knows where every one of his 2,000 sheep is, and what it is doing, at any given moment. He brings a whole new meaning to the New Testament references to good shepherds. I was not able to help much, except for providing moral support, but even so, Johnny's wife, Mary, always prudent, suggested I don a boiler suit. However, I was not prepared to deprive the nation of the sight of me in my purple cord breeches, canary-yellow stockings and spinach green tam-o'-shanter from Peggy MacSween of Scalpay, which Mary had bought me. I managed to keep my lower half moderately clean but no one who travelled in my car in Aberdeen the following week will ever forget the pungent smell of afterbirth on my loden jacket!

We only had one dawn shoot, but needless to say Johnny was out at 5.00 am every day. On

Ewes on their heft

the dawn shoot the weather was cold but stunning, and we had great fun, hearing the 'goback goback' call of the grouse, the strange whirr that I couldn't identify but which Johnny told me was made by a snipe's wing feathers, and over all the skylarks that reminded me of our childhood. Johnny is superb at his job. At one point we found a ewe with a lamb so awkwardly placed that he had to put the ewe over his shoulder to get the string round the lamb's horns (black-faced hill lambs have horns) before the lamb could be born. Johnny displayed all the tricks and miracles of his trade and even I, who know how good he is, was impressed. On the last day, after a week of fine weather, the heavens opened, proving that the weather at lambing isn't always, indeed seldom is, as kind as it had been for most of the filming of this programme.

The BBC troops departed, Mary took their son back to school and Johnny and I, fresh from welcome baths, sat and chatted happily. At 8.45 pm Johnny got up and said, 'I'm just going round the hill. You stay here and be comfortable.' I looked at the filthy night beyond the windows, got up and said, 'I'll just get my boots.' I don't suppose I helped much, but it was very companionable and it seemed churlish not to go out into the foul night with him.

On my fiftieth birthday, before any of these programmes were a reality, Johnny gave me a shepherd's crook that he had made himself. It is a thing of simple beauty with great feel appeal, and I love it dearly. It has a neck crook of simple horn on a hazel shaft, and it seems to me to give me extra street cred as a wannabe countryman. I ignore all Johnny's remarks about hookers! I knew that Johnny had studied with the great crook-maker, Donald Dickson, and it was to Donald that we went to film the craft. It is currently rumoured that due to the BSE scare Brussels is going to forbid the using of rams' horns for stick-making. I spoke to John Home Robertson, the Labour MP for East Lothian, to ask whether this was true. He denied it absolutely, which, if he is anything like the rest of them, probably means it is true.

Stick-making is an ancient craft. The ram's horn is cut to suit the natural curve and softened by heating it. It is then bent, in a clamp, into the required shape of either a neck or a leg crook, the latter being, of course, much narrower. Most neck crooks are dress crooks, to be carried with pride at shows, sales and fairs, and some of them are very elaborate indeed. Once the correct shape is reached, the head of the crook is painstakingly pared down to the stick-maker's own design, using a variety of rasps. It is then polished with the finest of glass papers. Any carving on the head (sheepdogs, thistles and pheasants are among the favourites) is done at this stage. Then the shaft is fitted, glued on and polished with shellac. There was one crook the like of which I hadn't seen before. The whole crook was made from a single piece of beech with only the head stripped and polished. The head of a crook can be varnished, painted or inlaid with bone. Buffalo horn, which is black, is imported in large quantities, and much of it goes into the stick-dressing industry.

The stick dressing is done in the old undercroft where once stalwart men in boiled leather

Stick-making, a dying art

jerkins and steel caps adjusted the straps on their bucklers and honed their broadswords. The beams were stacked with maturing shafts and there was an assortment of neatly stacked horn. It was a place of creation and industry and smelled of glue and dust. There waiting for me was Ali McGimpsey, Donald's friend and erstwhile pupil, a former miner from Tranent who had gone to one of Donald's stick-dressing classes and fallen for the art. The story-line was that I should make a stick for myself whilst Johnny went off to look at rabbit boxes. In the event Ali gave me a lovely leg crook which I used to great effect on camera.

Time and again one finds the men from the mining towns taking up country pursuits. They beat, pick up, rabbit and even escape to become keepers themselves. The dividing line here in the Lothians – and in many other parts of the British Isles – between Countrymen and Townies is very thin. Many Townies like me, once they know which way is up, leap over that line.

Donald farms in a sixteenth-century fortified farmhouse. When we arrived the yard was full of poultry. There were hens of all sorts, huge Marrons, Rhode Island Reds and, carefully caged away lest they crossbreed, his rare partridge portwine dots. There was a strutting bronze turkeycock and his mate, and Donald promised me one of their offspring for Christmas. All were happily pecking in the dust and demolishing some Brussels sprout stalks.

The spring sees the end of the hunting and country sporting season, and brings rebirth and regeneration. The farmers, their wives and families are hard at work after the fallow period of winter. However, all work and no play make Jack a dull boy and so point-to-pointing was born. And it was literally that: from point to point. Energetic young men rode across country taking their own line from one point (the start) to another easily visible point, usually a church steeple (the finish). From that cross-country events developed and so did steeplechasing: for which, originally, a church steeple was the goal. Point-to-pointing was almost certainly regulated by the

Point-to-pointing with the Fife Hunt

Hunt from the start, but this was first formalized in 1910 when a law was passed giving the organization of point-to-pointing to the Hunt. They were held on private land by the Hunt for the Hunt, and it wasn't until the period between the two world wars that the public were first admitted and charged an entrance fee.

Today the point-to-points are still managed by the Hunt. In order for a horse to qualify, it must have been hunted for seven days during the season immediately past with the relevant Hunt, and a certificate must be obtained to prove this fact, from the Hunt Secretary. The races are governed by the rules of the Jockey Club. The rules used to preclude not only professional jockeys, but also Hunt Servants, but these rules were relaxed with regard to the latter in 1932. Professional jockeys are still excluded. Ladies have always been allowed to race but only in Ladies' Races, until this rule was abolished in the 1960s. I only ever rode in one point-to-point in a Ladies' Race, and I have to say I have seen cleaner riding in an Australian bush track where they are noted for their skulduggery and dirty tricks. Nowadays point-to-points are big fund-raisers and many people go.

Esmé's friends, the Alexander brothers, are deeply involved in the Fife Hunt and so it was to that point-to-point that we went. It was a beautiful hot day and we were all in party mood after the exigencies of lambing. Johnny and I kept corpsing, and we weren't helped by Steve's efforts to imitate a horse so that we could follow the eye-line. At one time Esmé remarked resignedly to Robin, 'I suspect we have only another ten minutes of presenter concentration time left.' She was wrong by five minutes!

However, it was an opportunity for us to bid farewell to Mark Dradge, the Huntsman of the Fife. He is an interesting young man. He was born in a town and had no contacts with the country, yet he yearned, from a young age, to go into Hunt Service. He started in the kennels and worked his way up to Huntsman, and now he was off to the USA as Huntsman to the Midland. The Master had spotted him whilst on a trip to Scotland and offered him the job. He was taking his young wife and children with him and though he was excited by the adventure and the thought of the security offered (America has no problems with antis which is why some of them fund the International Fund for Animal Welfare to interfere over here), he was upset at the thought of missing seeing the progress in the hounds he had bred.

It was here that the Land Rover, which hadn't been that reliable throughout the programmes, finally breathed its last. It refused to start for dear Steve and rebuffed all the efforts of the AA to resuscitate it. I trust it isn't still sitting in a field in Fife.

CHAPTER SEVEN

NEGLIGENCE

On 8 May I left Tony, Ben and Shelley to cope with the lambing and took the red-eye from Dunbar to King's Cross. I used to love this four-hour journey to London. I would gradually unwind, read the papers, watch the countryside change, or simply spend the time jumping hedges. Now mobile telephones, the most obnoxious invention since barbed wire, make it a misery. I long to get hold of one of those electronic gadgets that jams the frequencies or, better still, travel everywhere with Clarissa. She manages to get away with threatening to throw the offending telephones out of the window.

London was absolutely sweltering and when I arrived at BBC White City employees were lying about the forecourt, basking like seals. London both attracts and appals me. I had a lot of fun there when I was younger but even then the claustrophobia used to get to me. After a while I had to move back to the country. The purpose of coming down so early was to interview a director for the last two programmes and from my point of view this represented something of a hiatus.

After five programmes we were working well together as a team. The technical branch, Robin and Shu on the cameras, were both proficient, intuitive, enthusiastic and always great fun. We hoped that Martin, who had fitted in so easily, would be able to stay as soundman. Steve was becoming a great friend. Chloë's ability to correlate our research material into highly efficient schedules and her eternal good humour made each day's filming run smoothly. Esmé had adapted to the unusual circumstances of the programmes being 'presenter-led' with enormous good grace and generosity of spirit. I suspected that this was by no means easy, and it was an indication of her professionalism that there was never any outward sign of how difficult it must have been.

Hating the thought of the status quo being disturbed, neither of us wanted her to leave, and ignorant of the enormous backlog of editing that had been building up, I could see no reason why she should. 'The woman's irreplaceable,' I said to myself grumpily, as I was stopped at the security barrier. 'Why, only the other day she expressed outrage at the gassing of nursing vixens in a manner that made me very proud.'

Where, I wondered, did the BBC expect to find another director with such sterling qualities?

Searching for a director with the necessary qualifications proved more difficult than expected and, while looking for one, the obvious was overlooked. Right under our noses was a highly experienced assistant producer who had been involved in the series from the beginning, and who was very much part of the team. To universal acclaim Chloë became our next director. Steve would continue with us on the shoots as Series Producer, and Esmé was able to edit the programmes and supervise the research. To use Clarissa's Caribbean expression, 'God no sleep.'

Our next stop was the Goodwood Park Hotel, where we were to stay for a dinner at Goodwood House hosted by Headline Book Publishing and the Booksellers Association. It was part of the annual Booksellers Association conference, which was taking place in Brighton. What with the traffic, and getting mildly lost near Midhurst, we only had time for a quick change before dashing up the drive towards Goodwood House itself. Our path was blocked by a fleet of double-decker buses.

'What the hell are buses doing here?' I asked Clarissa.

'Those,' she said, 'are the booksellers, arriving from Brighton.'

And so they were. All 300 of them, sustained during the long hot journey by unlimited champagne.

'What are we supposed to do?' I asked Clarissa.

'Chat up the booksellers,' she told me, surging into the throng, greeting acquaintances left and right. It was the most enormous fun. Headline and the Booksellers Association had really pushed the boat out. There was a damned good dinner, considering the numbers. My heroine, Barbara Windsor, presented prizes. Rolf Harris got 'em all going with the old chestnuts 'Tie me kangaroo down' and 'Waltzing Matilda', and showed an attractive young bookseller what the Aborigines really use a didgeridoo for. Louise Weir, Headline's Marketing Director, flitted about seeing that everything ran smoothly. Ros Ellis, Headline's Publicity Director, emerged from behind a pillar just as the attentions of two young ladies, who had dined unwisely and too well, were about to embarrass me. Altogether it was a terrific evening, with great interest shown in the forthcoming book.

The following morning over breakfast Clarissa, Heather Holden-Brown, Headline's Publishing Director, and I signed the book contracts. Being so far south, we decided on the spur of the moment to use the opportunity to drive down to the West Country and research material for the next programme. Fishing on the Tamar and its tributaries became a focal point for our continuing theme of farming, field sports and conservation. Our contact was a cousin of my Aunt Louise's – Anne Voss-Bark – who owns the famous fishing hotel, the Arundell Arms, at Lifton. Anne is deeply involved in river conservation issues and a trustee of the West Country Rivers Trust.

Fast shallows

Mink-hunting was the obvious choice of field sport and Louise Weir, who comes from that part of the world, put us in touch with Mark Prout of the Devon and Cornwall Mink-hounds. Clarissa's childhood friend from Sussex, Jo Coleman, would provide material on 'down-sizing'– dropping out for those of us who are not media literate – and organic farming at their farm near Bude in Cornwall.

Just before we left, Clarissa attended her old school reunion at The Sacred Heart in Hove. Here she ran into Lydia Burnet, who now lives near Lifton, hunts with the Lamerton, knows Mark Prout and proved to be a tremendous help to us. We flew westward in Clarissa's Saab convertible with the roof down in 24°C of brilliant sunshine. Moved by the spirit of the moment – it is not every day you sign your first book contract – Clarissa let me drive. This Saab is a beautiful piece of machinery, a perfect combination of power and high-tech engineering. Having spent most of my life in Land Rovers, driving it was like riding a thoroughbred after years on a cob.

I hadn't been down this way for a long time and we sped along, passing signposts that brought back many happy memories. Southampton, where I have caught the ferry so many times to the Isle of Wight, spending halcyon summer days at Bembridge and, in the winter, shooting high pheasants, glinting in the sunshine, somewhere near Carisbrooke Castle. Blandford, where I did my first and last parachute jump and where Bill Scott, my cousin and godfather, had been Master of the Portman after giving up the West Waterford. Past Dorchester and the sign to Yeovil where Aunt Louise lives, not far from the ghastly place where I was incarcerated for a bit, after I failed my Eton entrance, before I went to school in Switzerland. Round Exeter on the wrong side – it happens when we're nattering – and past the old A396 that winds its way through Tiverton and over Exmoor. Memories of cousin Martin's mastership of the Tiverton Foxhounds. Happy summers staying in the Crown at Exford and hunting with the Devon and Somerset Staghounds. Misty winter mornings hind-hunting in November. The indignity of being dispatched, at the age of fourteen, to the Porlock Vale School of Equitation for a month when it was run by Colonel Crawford, late the 10th Bengal Lancers and one of the most accomplished horsemen I have ever met. Thought I could ride, did I?

Skirting the edge of Dartmoor we arrived in Lifton and the Arundell Arms in time for tea. This really is a super place to stay: the epitome of an old-fashioned sporting hotel. It is very comfortable, runs like clockwork and the most superb grub cooked under the direction of Phillip Burgess, the chef, has earned the place an international reputation. We were in the middle of a grown-up discussion over who had eaten the most clotted cream when Clarissa's chum, Lydia, rolled up, full of enthusiasm and excitement for the programme, and offered to drive us over to the mink-hound kennels.

Mink are quite spectacularly horrible creatures. Their only redeeming feature is their luxurious pelt. Most predators kill selectively and, if they go on a killing spree, there is usually a reason for it. A mink will slaughter indiscriminately for the sheer wanton thrill of it – ask any poultry farmer what happens when one gets into his rearing pens. The devastation has to be seen to be believed. Mink were first imported to this country from America in the 1920s, for fur farming. A few escaped into the wild and a small breeding population was recorded in 1956. Since then, thanks largely to the antis and the other quasi-terrorist groups who attack mink farms and release mink, the population has now spread to all parts of Britain. A semi-aquatic creature, mink will

Devon and Cornwall Mink-hounds in action

destroy the fish population and surrounding river-bank wildlife wherever they become established.

Remember water voles? They are now virtually extinct because of mink, and the problem among colonies of sea birds in the Scottish Hebrides is so acute that the Mink Eradication Scottish Hebrides Scheme (MESH) has been set up to try to prevent them from colonizing North Uist from the islands of Lewis and Harris. We have them up here in Berwickshire, especially near where the feeder burns join the reservoir, and there are never any grouse or ground-nesting migratory birds along the bank sides. The bloody things live in or under the emergency hay sheds dotted about the hill, where sheep come down to shelter in rough weather. There is nothing more obnoxious than pulling out hay bales that mink have crapped all over on a freezing cold morning, and the sheep won't touch it. Mind you, we have had some thrilling days with the terriers when the sheds are cleared out in the summer. My old friend Donald has a couple of needle-sharp

Border-cross Patterdales that have got the job down to a fine art and learnt to work a mink from either end.

For over 800 years otters – considered vermin until they were sentimentalized by writers ignorant of the damage they did – were kept under control by otter-hound packs. During the Sixties and Seventies they gradually began dying out, killed by agricultural pesticides, particularly dieldrin, which accumulates in the tissues of their principal food source: fish and eels. This is a classic example of the damage scientists and the Ministry of Agriculture have done to our countryside. By the mid-Seventies the otter population was so small that many otter-hound packs had stopped culling otters and, early in 1977, the Masters of the Otter-hound Association passed a voluntary moratorium on hunting otters. This ended a piece of history that was first recorded in 1175, when Roger Follo was appointed 'King's Otter-Hunter' by a charter of Henry II.

In 1978, otters became a protected species by law in England and Wales, and throughout the British Isles in 1983. By now mink, whose varied diet protected them from poisoning by pesticides, were colonizing many of the habitats formerly occupied by otters, and hunting mink with hounds was proving the most effective means of control. Not only is it a free service available to farmers on request, but it is also far more successful than trapping.

Except for Masters of college beagle packs, Mark Prout is currently the youngest Master of Hounds. He became involved in Hunt Service on a voluntary basis after leaving school, when he started helping out John Underhill at the North Cornwall Kennels. John hunted the Devon and Cornwall Mink-hounds with the legendary Fred Darke in the summer as well, and Mark whipped-in to them. He then 'wasted eighteen months of my life', working in the Ambrosia factory at Lifton. In the run-up to the Hyde Park Rally on 10 July 1997, Mark applied for three weeks' leave to join other Hunt Supporters on their walk to London. Permission was refused, so Mark chucked in the job, worked out his notice and was in time to join the marchers at Salisbury. In London, footsore and triumphant, but jobless, he met John Underhill, who told him there was a position for him as kennelman and whipper-in with Tony Booth at the Lamerton.

'Strange, really,' he said. 'I walked to London not knowing what I was going to do next, and came away with an opportunity I had always wanted. A couple of months later I was whipping-in. I'd only been on a horse half a dozen times before.'

By 1998 John had given up mastership of the mink-hounds, and Mark was whipper-in to both the Lamerton and the North Cornwall Mink-hounds and, in 1999, he joined Darkie, who sadly died in 2000, as Joint Master. Eventually the winter work became too much and he gave up the Lamerton.

'I was skinning dead stock, for hound flesh, flat out for twelve hours on a Sunday, but there are not many people of my age who can say they've hunted hounds twelve months of the year the way I have for the last three years. I must see if I can find a beagle pack so I can keep it up.'

Mark now works for a firm of agricultural shed erectors, and kennels the ten couple of hounds in an adapted chicken-rearing shed. His home, a caravan, is parked nearby, following the old adage that a Huntsman should live close to his hounds.

Unable to reach him by telephone Clarissa, Lydia and I rolled up unannounced. We were received with great courtesy by Mark who padded happily about in his socks showing us his hounds: a mixture of otter-hound crosses and draft foxhounds. Two couple were distinctive black and tans from the Dumfriesshire.

'I've got just about the right combination of scent, voice and agility for the country,' he told us. 'It's big and varied.'

I asked how big.

'Pretty well everything west of Exeter,' he said.

Mark was dead keen to help with our programme and suggested we come down for a joint meet weekend with the Ytene Mink-hounds.

'We'll have a bit of hunting and a bit of a show on the Sunday. Nothing special, but we'll have some fun hopefully, if we don't get bothered by the antis.'

On the way back to the Arundell Arms I said to Clarissa, 'What a smashing chap, he really lives for his hunting, doesn't he?'

'Yes,' she mused, 'he is rather beautiful.'

'Why don't you grow up?' said Lydia.

That night Anne Voss-Bark described some of the problems that have led to the dramatic drop in salmon in the once-famous West Country rivers. She talked about the West Country Rivers Trust's efforts to try to repair the damage. A lot of it has to do with changes in agricultural policy, pollution and river-bank neglect. The Trust's 'Tamar 2000 Project' has been working in partnership with around 300 farmers, landowners and members of the wider community to improve the Tamar and its tributaries. Over 200 integrated farm management plans have already been drawn up, and nearly 400 kilometres of main rivers and tributaries has been surveyed. Thirty kilometres of river-bank fencing has been erected, sixty-two sites of severe erosion have been controlled, eighty spawning gravel sites have been de-silted and eight kilometres of river corridor woodland has been coppiced.

On Wednesday morning we drove to Endsleigh, the magnificent Regency cottage orné, built to designs drawn up by Sir Jeffrey Wyatt between 1811 and 1814 for the sixth Duke of Bedford. The house and grounds were the inspiration of Georgiana, the old boy's second wife, and are a classic example of the exquisite taste of that period. Endsleigh is positioned in a place of quite breathtaking natural beauty, overlooking the deep Tamar Valley, across to the thickly wooded Cornish bank. Humphry Repton, arguably the greatest landscape gardener, was roped in to transform the surroundings into a fantasy world of many secret gardens. There are rose walks

and terraces that lead to summer-houses and grottoes, paths to hidden dells and crags. An arboretum, planted with a wonderful combination of colours, includes Indian horse chestnuts, Norman firs, Himalayan birches, Japanese cedar, weeping beeches, Persian ironwoods and tiger-tail spruces. There are lily-ponds, cascades and acres of rhododendrons, azaleas and camellias. On a warm May morning the panorama, birdsong, colours and scents were almost overpowering.

It was an extraordinary experience visiting Endsleigh again. My grandparents used to take the fishing here in the early Sixties, when Horace Adams was water bailiff, and my parents brought me down with them one summer holiday. Nothing seemed to have changed in the house. The dark panelled hall and faded grandeur of the drawing-room were just as I remembered them. There was the very rhododendron bush into which my father had reversed, breaking a magnificent twelve foot split cane Hardy he had laboriously assembled and strapped to the roof of his car. Disappointingly, he only said, 'Damn'. Here were the paths and terraces to the Shell House and Swiss Cottage along which I had scampered; the Dairy Dell where I lay in the long grass watching the brown trout jump, hoping to see an otter. There were the stables and tack-room with the musty smell of old leather and the Cascade tumbling down to the Tamar, where I would sit for hours watching my father cast, mesmerized by the flow of water and the hiss of his line.

Anne had arranged for us to meet Bob Wellard, the water bailiff, who would show us some of the improvements and riverside rehabilitation that had been completed with the assistance of

ABOVE: Black Roar at Endsleigh
LEFT: Endsleigh: Georgiana's dream

the West Country Rivers Trust. As we drove along in his Land Rover beside the Tamar, he outlined some of the problems affecting salmon stocks, which have fallen to 20% of their numbers since the Seventies, and the effect that this has had on the local economy. It is a depressing catalogue, some of which can be ameliorated with help from the Trust, some will require legislation. Factory ships drift-netting off the west coast of Ireland decimate salmon stocks that are making for inland waters. Licensed netting at the estuaries accounts for still more.

'It is ridiculous,' Bob told us as we stopped to inspect a stretch of river-bank, previously trodden bare by watering cattle, now protected by a new buffer fence and growing a mass of wild flowers, 'that in this day and age none of the licencees make their living from netting. A rod-caught salmon is worth £7,000 to the local economy when you take into account the tourist infrastructure dependent upon fly-fishing. A netted salmon is worth £2.20p per kilogram to the netters.'

Driving on, Bob pointed out areas of recent coppicing. 'Excessive bank-side growth leads to over-shading and often to bank erosion. We get terrific spates after heavy rainfall. The soil around the tree roots gets washed away and eventually the tree comes down, taking a large chunk of the bank with it. Too much shade also leads to a loss of the bank-side vegetation that strengthens river-banks. Too little leads to high water temperatures. Coppicing can achieve the desired mix of both and the wood taken out has a value to the farmer, or riparian owner, if only as firewood.'

The Tamar tumbled along, dark chocolate brown in colour. Bob explained the reason for this, and the problems it created. Starting at Bude and dividing Cornwall from Devon, the Tamar runs through farm land that used to be predominantly grazing land. Due to the infamous BSE scare and upheavals in the dairy industry, many farmers have switched to arable production. Others are making silage from maize and, in both instances, topsoil gets washed into the Tamar. Silt, settling into the gravel beds, makes the outer surfaces too hard for salmon to wriggle into when

The eighteenth-century cockpit, now the rod room at the Arundell Arms Hotel

they are trying to spawn, and the eggs simply get washed away. In other areas eggs are smothered by silt in the redds. In some places egg survival has been as low as 2%. In the winter of 1999 the West Country Rivers Trust, in conjunction with the Environment Agency and the Tamar and Tributaries Fishing Association, carried out successful artificial egg-rearing trials. They planted fertile eggs in gravel on specially constructed boxes which were designed to ensure that the flow of water kept the eggs free of silt.

Further along the river, opposite a cliff face rising sheer from the water where a peregrine nests annually, Bob showed us a wetlands area buffer zone. This stretch of boggy, rush-covered land, several yards back from the river-bank, had been created to act as a filter for the nitrates that are washed off it. Bacteria in wetlands perform a denitrification process: they convert nitrates into harmless nitrogen gases. The buffer zones also act as a sponge after heavy rainfall: they reduce flooding, and assist with trapping topsoil and farm slurry, and provide reserve grazing in droughts. There is also the added bonus – everyone's dream come true – a potential snipe bog.

It had been a fascinating morning in the company of someone whose knowledge of fishing and passion and enthusiasm for the Trust had been inspiring. After lunch at the Arundell Arms we met Roy Buckingham, the hotel's head bailiff, in the rod room, one of the few remaining ancient cockpits in existence. Roy took us on a tour of some of the hotel's extensive fishing beats on the tributaries leading into the Tamar, on which they also have some fishing.

The hotel runs extremely popular fishing courses and part of the tuition is held in an old, flooded lime quarry with water so clear you can see the brown and rainbow trout. Roy reminded me of a huntsman showing hounds, as he scattered handfuls of fish feed, bringing them to the surface in a feeding frenzy. From there we went on a magical trip down narrow, high-banked Devon lanes covered with bluebells, flowering wild garlic, pink campion, periwinkles and cow parsley. We stopped periodically to look at beats on the Lyd, Wolf, Ottery and Thrushel. These were enchanted places, a fly-fisherman's paradise. There were deep secret pools, shaded by oak, ash and sycamore; gravelly runs and stickles; banks where fruit bushes, washed down in the floods, had self-rooted; open glides and fast shallows. Roy pointed out places where cattle had widened and damaged the banks, and he talked of his hopes for the improvements that the Trust could make along the tributaries. It was a wonderful afternoon: we only wished we had brought our own rods but 'the general public are fascinated by pigs,' we had been told, and so it was to a pig farm that we went.

The day before Johnny and I were about to embark on this next adventure I went to an old school reunion and there I saw my friend Lydia, who lives near Lifton. After the publishers' dinner, where to my great delight I met that great trouper Barbara Windsor, we pressed on to the Arundell Arms. I rang Lydia who came over for a cup of tea and took us to meet Mark.

Hello!

We also discussed with her what else we could look for in the area and she told us about a family who had a pig farm where the pigs were fed almost exclusively on the waste from the Ambrosia Creamed Rice factory. Ambrosia aren't joking when they claim their product is made in the heart of Devon: the factory stands four square in the centre of Lifton and is one of the main employers in the area. It was from here that Mark set out to march to London in 1997.

We were in holiday mood, the sun shone, Johnny's lambing was over and all was going well at present. I wish you could have seen Johnny (indeed I wish Johnny could have seen himself) in a pair of stylish white stockman's jeans that his son had grown out of, Chelsea boots with a red snuff handkerchief tumbling out of his back pocket (ignoring all my warnings that he'd be picked up) and tanned from the journey. He looked every inch a television presenter. The expression on his face when the water bailiff said wistfully, 'I expect you have lots of girlfriends', kept me in stitches for a week.

After a day looking at rivers Lydia came and took us to the pig farm. There were four generations living and working on the farm, from Grandma who lived in her stone keep, to a sturdy three year old with a hoe. Johnny's beauty was not lost on Grandma who whisked him off to her keep and offered him a bowl of custard, but she walks the farm like Diogenes with a bucket of swill, looking for an honest pig who isn't a custard junkie.

The family have to collect the tins and cartons of creamed rice, custard and sometimes even pasta sauce from the factory, but I feel this is no great hardship in return for all the free food they receive. The lorry is unloaded into the crushing shed – they have bought a crusher from Heinz which literally squashes the containers until they burst – and the food drains away into vats where it is mixed with barley grown on the farm. The tanks are then connected to the distribution machinery and a

'Empress of Blandings'

Heath Robinson pumping device carries the food to the feeding troughs. Buttons are pushed, lights flash and there is then a great cranking, spluttering noise followed by a sound like a high-speed jet revving up and taking off. At this sound the pigs, who have been mooching about in a pig-like way, prick up their ears and sidle closer to the troughs.

Suddenly the food whizzes along the connecting tubes and into the feeders, and the pigs zip into action in one huge concentrated movement. 'Phlp', and every head is in the trough as one. They fight if there isn't room, but of course it's the greediest pig that goes to market soonest for once they reach the required weight, off they go. I observed that the young boars still had their knackers on and was told that, as they go to market at fourteen weeks, there is no need to castrate them: they are too young for the taste of the meat to be affected. The uncastrated male of any animal has a strong, rather rank taste caused by the male hormones, and is not good eating. Consequently, unless a male animal is being kept for breeding purposes (and only the very best are), it is castrated young so that the meat is fit for food. Meat with a good covering of fat cooks well, doesn't dry out and tastes considerably better. This is particularly true of pork which, without fat, becomes very indigestible. The crackling doesn't cook so well and the taste is non-existent.

If the Meat and Livestock Commission wants a pig industry in this country it must re-educate itself, and the public, and help the farmers to rebuild. The Government health advisers suffer from tunnel vision and, having grasped a mildly good idea, ride it to death without stepping back to look at the wider picture. I am rendered virtually speechless by the state of the pork industry. It is almost impossible to buy fat pork except from specialist suppliers such as Peter Gott at Sillfield Farms, or Jan McCourt at Northfield Farms. Pigs are meant to be fat, they produce it with consummate ease: PG Wodehouse's 'Empress of Blandings' is the role model for pigs. A couple of years ago I bought two two-year-old Tamworths raised on the best organic produce, but I had huge trouble finding an abattoir to kill them because of their size. For years we have been troubled by bacon that is tasteless and pumped full of water to increase its weight, so that when you buy supermarket bacon you are buying 25% water which runs into your frying-pan as white slime.

Everybody blames everybody else for the situation. My researcher, Henrietta Palmer, who behaves like a good terrier when in pursuit of a fact, rang round the producers, the slaughterers and the supermarkets. The supermarkets blamed the customers, but where are these customers? Of all the hundreds of people I have met in the last few years, not one has said, 'How wonderful it is that we get such lean pork'. The abattoirs say that the supermarkets demand that the fat be trimmed or they will not pay their bills, and the producers say that the abattoirs discount their pigs if there is any excess fat which they have to trim. The abattoirs are happy because they have smaller carcasses to handle, the farmers are trapped by the demands of the supermarkets and the supermarkets, who stick the word 'Healthy' on everything, make yet more money. The people who produce fat pigs say that every time they send a load to slaughter they end up missing half a pig – condemned for bruising – but half a pig is enough for some very good dinners, so obviously the slaughterers still know which meat is good enough to keep!

In Northern Ireland I hear the abattoirs are refusing coloured pigs, such as Gloucester Old Spots, Saddlebacks, Essex and Berkshires. The rational for this is that the supermarkets will not take pork with marked skin in case it is really bruising, as if one couldn't tell the difference. I feel that another reason is that the older breeds tend to be bigger and the abattoirs don't like them. Small abattoirs allow the farmer to track an individual beast right through the system and are usually nearer the home farm. The Government is supermarket-driven in wanting to close down the small abattoirs: one big supermarket chain takes its beasts from all over the British Isles to Devon to be slaughtered. Imagine the hardship this causes, and it is a real blow for the rarebreeds' producers. Thank God then for the Small Abattoir Foundation.

The real villain of the piece, it emerges, is the Meat and Livestock Commission. Government bodies have medical advisers, and the medics get it wrong most of the time. My father was an extremely prominent member of that profession and he used to say, 'Remember how Charles II died? He died of the worst excesses of the best doctors of the day. They put boiling pigeon dung on the soles of his feet, and anointed his shaved head with the urine of young babies. We haven't progressed very much farther, we simply package it better.'

Anyway, thirty years ago the Government medics decided that the real killer was animal fat and they started laying down specifics for leaner and leaner meat. The supermarkets, eager to win customers from traditional butchers, jumped on the bandwagon. Funny ain't it: cigarette manufacturers and alcohol producers pay huge subsidies to the Government so they aren't railed against, and supermarkets give huge campaign gifts to the various parties, as do fast-food chains. Draw your own conclusions. In the meantime the heart-attack rate continues to rise and, as the only natural stimulator of serotonin is animal fat, more and more people take to Prozac and other antidepressants. I have a theory that it is the fat content in burgers that makes them so popular because it is elsewhere absent from the diet. Even if the demand for lean pork was originally customer-led – by customers who bought the 'animal fat is bad for you' line – most of those customers soon realized that they didn't like the bland, and indigestible, product that resulted and so they stopped buying it. There are no longer enough customers and the result is that the pork industry in this country is falling into rack and ruin, and the poor pigs, far from having a happy life out-of-doors, get sunburnt because they have no fat to protect them.

I discussed all this with the family who said that they simply have no choice in the matter. The bulk of their pork goes to supermarkets and supermarkets demand lean pork. The pigs thrive well in their short lives on their strange diet. I asked why there was so much of this food available: apparently all the products are X-rayed and the slightest burnt skin or imperfection is discarded, also the supermarkets demand a clear two-year sell-by date on tinned goods, so I saw cans being crushed that read: 'Best before 2001'.

With the exception of Grandma, the family live in a modern bungalow on the farm. One daughter is the head of the local Young Farmers Association, and plays the organ beautifully in the local parish church. The family are an energetic and imaginative part of the community and, like the Larkins, the very sort that the bureaucrats would love to abolish. They manage to continue in the pig-farming business, unlike so many others in the British Isles, because the food that their pigs eat costs them nothing. Most other pig farmers are not so lucky.

Mark Prout took his mink-hounds to clear mink from the family's trout hatchery. Because mink are semi-aquatic, their scent is both on the river-banks and on the water. This means that mink-hounds spend as much time in the water as they do on land. We then went to have a look at a small holding. My friend Christine (remember Chapter One?) has a sister called Josephine, and she and her husband James have down-sized – the term applied to people who leave the world of commerce to farm small holdings. James was a successful commercial lawyer and practised in Hong Kong, Singapore and finally London. Hankering for the country, they bought

ABOVE: Have you heard the one about...
RIGHT: A South Devon and a downsizer

East Penrost Farm near Launceston in Cornwall. It is an eighty-acre holding which they farm organically. They have also adapted one of their barns and made an extremely stylish and comfortable place to rent out to visitors, complete with a website which is full of information about the life of the farm. They have some Lleyn sheep (pronounced clean) and some Soay and some others, some Red Devon cattle, hens for eggs and everything a countrywoman could desire. At the wedding of their only daughter, a naval officer, to a submariner, I talked to their eldest son, Thomas, whom I have known and liked since he was small. He was raised for a great deal of his life in urban luxury but now, just leaving university, he spoke with such love of the land and farming: all he wants to do now is farm with his parents. He is a countryman at heart.

As the evening went on we barbecued a couple of lambs from a neighbour, straight off Dartmoor: just cooked, carved and served in a bun with a dash of mint sauce (that last vestige of the Crusades). The meat was succulent and sweet with the taste of the upland herbs that they graze on: no butcher's lamb this, fattened on roots and processed feed, but lamb as it should taste and utterly irresistible. Later that night I picked my way to the caravan parked by the lambing sheds, where I was to sleep, only to discover that I had no bedding. I shivered my way fitfully

until dawn. After waking Jo's sister, Christine, and my godson, I sped north again to continue working on this book.

As I drove I thought about the Colemans' Lleyn sheep. Sometime during our filming Johnny had told me about a man on Anglesey who had bred a sheep which did not need shearing because it shed its coat in small clumps. This piece of information naturally alerted the cynic in me. I have spent a lot of my life being mobbed up by Johnny because of my ignorance on country matters. I still remember, painfully, the hoots of laughter which followed my enquiring why his ferrets were making so much noise one spring. I blush to think that I believed the given explanation rather than the obvious one. I grind my teeth at the thought that I really believed that the terrible smell, as one climbed the Downs at Bo Peep, was caused by sheepskins fermenting to produce an alcoholic drink that was exported to Russia, rather than by the quail farm. So you can see why I doubt 'clean sheep'. This doubt was exacerbated by the fact that I couldn't find the Lleyn Peninsula on the map (until, maddeningly, Johnny pointed it out to me: it's in north -west Wales). Unlikely, too, was the description of a cross between a Welsh White and a Wiltshire Woodland with a touch of Shetland. With glee I informed Johnny that Jo's Lleyn sheep had to be sheared.

'Ahh.' He paused meditatively. 'But are they pure.'

I have now developed a total paranoia about Lleyn sheep and when I ask people if they know about them, and they assure me they do exist, I am convinced Johnny's just talked to them and told them to toe the line. Help from anyone out there with self-shearing Lleyn (or even dirty) sheep would be much appreciated. Please get in touch!

Interestingly, because of down-sizing, land prices haven't dropped despite the appalling and continuing recession in the farming industry, thus creating a false picture for the Government to focus on. It has always been the case in the British Isles that men make their pile in the City, then buy a country estate, and farming recessions, of course, pressurize existing holders – who have fallen on hard times – to sell. But this phenomena used to be peculiar to the large estates. Down-

This is an elephant, children!

sizing applies to much smaller land holdings, like Jo and James's, of about eighty acres. Organic farming, which is done on a much smaller scale, and the growth of the 'Farm Experience' for tourists from the towns, has made this way of things viable.

For years many small farms have offered bed and breakfast during the tourist season but, with the widening divide between town and country, even a cow being milked, or the sight of a chicken, is perhaps more of a peculiarity than the rare beasts in the zoos or on our television screens. Many Townie children have seen an elephant but not a sheep. So, by offering a little more insight into how a farm works, the prudent farmer gains not only rental but, sometimes, a little unpaid labour to help with his chores. My enquiries disclosed that one agency alone has 1,500 farms on their books that offer the farm experience.

The growth of Farmers' Markets also aid this type of farming, as there is a ready local outlet for fresh produce and instant income for the farmer. As patron of the Farmers' Markets Association, and a fighter for this cause for many years, I am delighted at their increase. It is a movement that is enormously strong in America and should decrease the divide between town and country. If the urbanite can speak to the farmer face to face, maybe the tensions and misunderstandings will be eased. Farmers' Markets, where all the produce has to come from within a twenty-mile radius (forty in London), supply the perfect outlet to the small organic

A Farmers' Market — an increasingly popular way to shop

producer, and it is interesting to note that vegetables at such markets sell out amazingly quickly. The other outlet for organic vegetables is box schemes, but these are much more time-consuming for the producer. And no small producer wants to become embroiled with the maw of the supermarkets, and there are not yet enough organic shops.

The main difficulty for the vegetable producer is to overcome the brainwashing that this generation has received about cosmetic appearance. Supermarkets have ruined the vegetable trade by demanding visual conformity at the cost of taste. People need to be re-educated so that they understand how vegetables grow: they do not grow, naturally, in uniform shapes. But they taste delicious when they haven't been pumped full of water and nitrates just to make them more colourful. Organic meat is a different matter: specialist suppliers want all the good stuff they can buy and the public are better educated about organic meat, particularly post-BSE. Anne Petch at Heal Farm, with her rare breeds' meat, or Pipers Farms, where a whole valley in Devon is now given over to the proper production of food, are well in the vanguard of the current trend, and their experience shows that there is money in 'them thar hills' for the small producer. Anyone who has been to one of Henrietta Green's Food Lovers' Fairs knows how fast things are growing in this sector. I did not really believe that organic would work, but the market is flourishing and expanding and I am glad to have been proved wrong. But there's still a long row to hoe.

CHAPTER EIGHT

FOLLY

J Every few years there is a perfect May and this millennium year was one of them: day after day of brilliant sunshine, with just enough warmth to make the grass grow and provide insect life for the grouse chicks to feed on for the first few days of life, before they become veggies and move on to young heather shoots. Racing to meet the deadline, 26 June, for the first seven chapters of this book, we hardly saw any of it. For the first time in my farming life, I was trapped in the house, clutching a hot pencil. Outside I could see Tony on the quad-bike as he went round checking the ewes and lambs.

Clarissa zoomed backwards and forwards from one end of the country to the other, meeting her incredible schedule of commitments, and, in between, she hauled out her laptop to type. Meanwhile, somewhere in a hot and dusty London, Steve was locked into an edit suite, editing hours of footage filmed during the week of the Waterloo Cup. In a tiny sweltering room at the top of BBC Scotland, in Edinburgh, Chloë painstakingly logged the lambing programme, a process that involves assessing and annotating every piece of footage. In the bowels of the building, surrounded by television screens, Esmé and Jan, the editor,

Terry large, falconer

worked on the second edit of the Mull programme.

On 6 June I joined Clarissa in Cheshire where she was demonstrating at a food fair at Tatton Park. We stayed the night nearby and went to see Johnnie O'Shea, who trains our greyhounds. The start of the coursing season was only twelve weeks away and under Johnny's training and care the dogs were looking magnificent. Our new pup, whom we hoped to race for the first time this season, had grown like a mushroom.

The next day we set off to research the programme on Wales. The central issue was to be the plight of the Welsh grouse moors, how the grouse population had dwindled away and what was being done to build it back up again. Many of the problems stem from predators amongst which are the carrion crows who take grouse eggs and chicks at hatching time. We had arranged to meet Terry Large, a falconer, on Denbigh Moor the following day, but had decided to base ourselves at the West Arms in Llanarmon initially, and just do a general reconnaissance on our first afternoon.

The West Arms had been recommended, and Llanarmon had been suggested as a picturesque part of the world. It is situated in the upper reaches of the River Ceiriog, not far from the spectacular Ceiriog Falls, in a green fertile valley surrounded by rolling hills leading up to wild empty moors. It is an area steeped in history, with an Iron Age fort on Mynydd, above the village, which must at one time have been occupied by the Romans. A hoard of coins dating from that period was found nearby in the Twenties. In 1165, Henry II's invading army was soundly thrashed by Prince Owen of Gwynned and many of the dead were buried at Adwyr Beddai. From time to time, over the centuries, the valley has had little bursts of prosperity with fulling mills, flannel manufacture, slate and chinastone quarrying. Always wonderful sheep country, the area has reverted to being almost entirely agricultural, deriving extra income from tourism in the summer and shooting in the winter. The topography of the landscape lends itself to high sporting pheasants.

After a splendid tea of Welsh scones, Clarissa and I decided to go for a walk. Llanarmon is indubitably a lovely place but, at virtually the end of the B4500, I was beginning to wonder whether it wasn't perhaps a little limited from a research point of view, when Clarissa said, 'Look, a man with a shotgun. Let's ask him what he's up to.'

'Pigeon flighting?' I queried.

'No,' he said. 'The keeper's putting hounds through the woodlands round here before the pheasants are released. We're just going up to the kennels. We saw you at the Waterloo Cup. Come and join us.'

Clarissa's magnificent royal blue Saab convertible joined the growing cavalcade of Land Rovers and farm pick-ups winding their way out of Llanarmon towards Pensarn. After half a mile we stopped at a neat modern bungalow where ten couple of foxhounds were being loaded into a van. We moved on again to a block of woodland. Followers with shotguns positioned themselves at intervals round the wood. The Huntsman took his hounds into the wood and someone with a lurcher climbed the bank overlooking the opposite side. This was a traditional Welsh 'shooting' pack and a tremendous piece of good luck for us. Not only were we in for an evening's sport, it was one of the methods of predator control that we would be filming on the Denbigh Moors.

Clarissa and I spent a fascinating evening with the Llanarmon. Shooting packs have to adapt their method of hunting to the terrain. In thick wooded cover, hounds hunt the fox towards waiting guns, rather like the old Saxon method of driving quarry towards a party of armed hunters. Sometimes hounds are assisted by a much faster gaze-hound in the form of a lurcher, like the Normans used to hunt with, and on open moorland where the use of firearms is very

End of the day for the Llanarmon pack

limited, hounds hunt in the traditional manner. On some days and in certain areas hounds are ridden to, on others, hunted on foot.

There is more hunting per square mile in Wales than in any other part of the British Isles, and it plays an enormous role in rural areas where agricultural incomes are largely from sheep. Hunting here is different from the rest of the British Isles. It involves a mixture of control methods which have evolved according to the locality and terrain. Some are the traditional mounted packs, some are foot packs similar to the fell packs of the Lake District, and some are 'shooting' packs like the one we joined. These have emerged over the last forty years as a result of massive forestry plantations. The most significant change in the nature of the Welsh countryside was caused by the planting of vast tracts of land. These plantations became havens for predators, particularly foxes. Within a short period of time, fox predation became a major problem to sheep farmers and, especially after myxomatosis destroyed the rabbit population, accelerated the decline of ground-nesting birds, particulary red grouse.

As a result, in many areas, groups of farmers and others with an interest in hunting began to acquire a few foxhounds which could be hunted in an informal way as and when required by the farmers and landowners. Hounds were fed and kennelled by local volunteers and in the summer individual hounds would be 'trencher fed' by local farmers. So effective have these small packs become that many have expanded and are funded by contributions from the farming community and funds raised by local social events, village dances, hunt auctions and dinners. Some hunts are now big enough to employ a part-time Huntsman, others continue as they started, being wholly run by volunteer support. The number of packs has increased dramatically in the last twenty years with the ever-growing fox population, most of which are feral, but a number are urban foxes caught in the towns and dumped in the countryside. This is a problem that is escalating in many rural areas.

As fox-hunting with hounds is carried out over virtually the whole of rural Wales, the need for a governing body to unite and represent organized hunting had been the subject of debate for several years. In 1997 the Federation of Welsh Hill Packs was formed which provides rigid but workable codes of conduct, enhanced by their membership of the Independent Supervisory Authority for Hunting, and now represents some forty-eight packs of hounds. An interesting cultural aspect that illustrates the importance of hunting in this area is the difficulty the Welsh media have in finding Welsh speakers to appear in programmes or debates against field sports. Welsh is the language of these rural areas where field sports are central to the way of life.

That night, after dinner, we joined Vic Matthews, the Master, and some of the fifty or so followers who had been out that evening, in the bar of the West Arms. Vic is also the local keeper and, apart from using his hounds to help him with vermin control on his employer's estate, he provides a vital service to the farming community. Earlier that day, the Government had announced, in a knee-jerk reaction to back-bench pressure, that it now intended to introduce a Bill to ban field sports. New Labour may be too arrogant to look to history and see what happened the last time a government ignored the countryside, and we had a civil war, but had they been in the pub that night they would have been terrified by these Welsh countrymen's calm acceptance of the battle to come. When a Welshman says, in that quiet threatening way, 'Right boyo', you know it's time to look out.

On Wednesday 14 June we set off across Wales for our meeting with Terry Large at a pub called the Sportsman's Arms on the Denbigh Moors. Clarissa was on sparkling form.

Llanarmon Foxhounds with Vic Matthews

'Here,' she said magnanimously, 'you drive.' No greater love hath the owner of a Saab 900 convertible than to allow another to drive it occasionally.

'I shall map-read.'

I felt a prickle of disquiet. Clarissa has always doubted the competence of the Ordnance Survey Department. Passable cartographers they might be, but when it comes to getting from A to B, she can always come up with her own improvements. Terry's directions had been perfectly succinct. Follow the A5 and turn off onto the A543. All might have been well if we had stuck to these instructions, but Clarissa was studiously poring over the map, always an ominous sign.

'Got it,' she announced triumphantly. 'A short cut. Save lots of time. Turn left here.'

Half an hour later we arrived in a muddy farmyard. Miraculously Terry was still waiting for us at the Sportsman's Arms when we finally rolled up three-quarters-of-an-hour late. I was about to launch into profuse apologies, but Clarissa got in first.

'I don't think much of your directions, Terry. Lucky I had the *Good Pub Guide* with me or we would have been back in Chester.'

Steven Lea, the press officer for BASC, hearing that we wanted to show how hawks can be used to control predators, had put me in touch with Terry. We subsequently discovered that Terry was a great friend of Vinnie Faal and had been an enormous help to a friend of mine who has recently taken up falconry, another example of the countryside network. Terry is one of those remarkable people who are able to combine running a successful business, whilst at the same time working tirelessly for the Countryside Alliance. After being made redundant in 1992 he decided to utilize his skills as a falconer and encyclopaedic knowledge of hawks to set up his own company: Terry Large Falconry Displays. During the summer he holds falconry courses, attending corporate days and county shows around the country. He shares his experience of the countryside and love of birds of prey with the crowds that flock to hear something about the ancient and noble art of falconry. During the winter he arranges for individuals to spend time with experienced

Learning about the countryside

falconers and can also offer falconry as an alternative to shooting, slipping his hawks onto game-birds. He was involved in establishing and promoting the Campaign for Falconry and currently acts as national co-ordinator for the various regions of the Countryside Alliance.

Somehow, he finds time to give talks and lectures on the countryside to groups ranging from large societies to small schools. Educating the young is an area of paramount importance to the future of the countryside, and one that we were particularly eager to film. After a school visit, Terry arranges for the school children to join him for a hands-on country sports day, run in conjunction with the Countryside Alliance. Here, many children from urban areas are given the opportunity to try fly-fishing, target-shooting with air rifles, ferreting, pony-riding and basic pony care, feeding and tacking up. Usually, the huntsman of the local Hunt will bring hounds to the venue, or the children are taken on a visit to the kennels. They go on estate walks and visit a keeper to see the pheasant hatcheries and rearing pens, followed by a short talk on his way of life and his role in the conservation of the countryside.

One of the aspects explained by Terry is how the British countryside, with its woods and hedges, has been shaped by field sports. Up to a certain altitude above which trees don't grow naturally, the whole of the British Isles was covered in forest. Gradually trees were cut down to make room for agriculture to feed the ever-expanding population. As the trees disappeared, so did the wildlife that lived in the forests. Specific areas of woodland were left as game cover. Except for commercial blocks of conifer forestry, new planting is carried out to replace old game cover or to create new ones. All farmland has two values: one is its agricultural potential, the other sporting. In some places the second is more valuable than the first. Without the sporting value it would not have been in a farmer's or landowner's economic interest to keep and maintain small, attractive areas of woodland, hedgerows and copses for the benefit of both game and other wildlife.

Terry explains the role of the predator in the countryside – the old story of the survival of the fittest and how field sports play their part in the management of wildlife. How a balance between all species is maintained by selective culling. He demonstrates this by using the children and the teachers in a form of role-play. A larger child chases and catches a smaller one: they represent a fox and a rabbit. A quick, healthy child given a good start and chased by a group of other children represent the fox and hounds. The 'fox' will usually escape. Their teacher, in the same situation, unless he or she is a keep-fit fanatic, inevitably gets caught. This role-play is very popular, as is the one to demonstrate how, in match coursing under National Coursing Club rules, the aim is to provide a fair challenge to competing greyhounds. Terry is the slipper, two children are the greyhounds, another child is the hare. The fit hare always outstrips the greyhounds, but a teacher in the same circumstances rarely does and there is no competition. The purpose of match coursing under NCC rules is to provide a challenge to two greyhounds, not to kill the hare. The day ends with an open discussion to look at the different field sports, and how these influence conservation

Mine's bigger than yours

in the countryside. With the wisdom of hindsight I know we all wish more had been done to educate 'the man on the Clapham omnibus', but no one knew then quite how wide the gap between town and country was becoming each year until politicians started to capitalize on it.

Terry had brought with him Major Tom Smith, the Chairman of the Countryside Alliance for North Wales, who has shooting rights over 7,000 acres of the moors, and Bob Williams, the keeper. The view across Denbigh Moors is breathtaking. Just behind the Sportsman's Arms is the ruin of a curious house, Gwylfa Hiraethog, the Watch Tower of the Hiraethog mountains. It was built by Hudson Ewbanke Kearney, later Viscount Devonport, at the end of the last century as a shooting lodge when the Denbigh Moors were productive grouse moors. The lodge, big enough to house a shooting party and servants, was made in Norway entirely of wood, shipped across, and a team of Norwegians struggled to erect it in the windiest part of North Wales. At over 1,600 feet, before it was abandoned and fell down, the house was the highest private dwelling in the British Isles and had the most wonderful view. On a clear day the whole of the spectacular Snowdon range with Snowdon itself, Moel Siabod and Moel Fammaw are visible, forty miles away, as is the Irish Sea to the north west. Occasionally, after a storm when the atmosphere is clear, the Isle of Man, the mountains of Mourne in Ulster and the Mull of Galloway can be seen. Apparently there was no garden and the heather was encouraged to grow right up to the house.

Cock grouse would sometimes perch on the front steps calling 'goback, goback'. The house was abandoned in the 1920s and sheep now shelter in the ruins of the principal rooms.

Major Tom had kindly agreed to allow us to use his moor to demonstrate the plight of the red grouse in Wales, the reasons for their disappearance and the efforts being made to bring them back. Predator control is an essential part of moorland management and, among other things, we intended to film Phil Lloyd with his Siabod pack of hounds, consisting of foxhounds, spaniels and lurchers, and Terry Large hawking for carrion crows.

Those of us who farm in the hills know the carrion crow as a brutal creature. A pair of crows circling over the moor at lambing time, or before we shear the sheep in the summer, indicates that something is in danger. Sometimes the shape of a sheep's fleece makes rolling over and regaining its feet difficult. This is the time a carrion crow will swoop down and, landing nearby, wait patiently until the sheep's struggles get weaker before hopping close enough to start work on its eyes. In the spring, when they are nesting, the eggs and chicks of other birds are particularly vulnerable. If all else fails, carrion crows feed off any dead animals. They are extremely wary of humans and, with their exceptional eyesight, very difficult to approach. The only time we are able to exercise some form of control is at nesting time, when baited larsen traps catch a certain number. For the rest of the year they have the free run of the place, unless there is a falconer nearby with the right sort of hawk.

Gotcha! A crow succumbs to a larsen trap

Falconry is an incredibly ancient form of field sport, probably as old as coursing. The Assyrians, Persians and Egyptians trained and flew hawks as did the Romans, Saxons and Normans. Marco Polo, reporting a hunt of the Kublai Khan in 1298, mentions that among the vast retinue were a great number of falconers to fly hawks at waterfowl. The Crusaders met falconers in the Middle East who had taken the art to a level far beyond their own. They brought back an entirely new degree of sophistication and elegance, as well as exotic new breeds. During the age of chivalry, falconry developed a language of its own, which every page had to learn. To use this language incorrectly was the worst form of social solecism. In the rigid stratification of the age, a grading of hawks according to the social rank of the owner came into being. Peregrines were the prerogative of the great and the good. Merlins were for ladies, goshawks for yeomen, sparrowhawks for priests and kestrels, which are only capable of catching mice, were for uncouth knaves or servants. Falconry remained enormously popular, both as a sport and a means of filling the larder. It was, after all, the only effective way of catching birds on the wing until the seventeenth century, when a type of shotgun was developed and the hawk became redundant.

Thankfully for the skilled mystery of hawking, a few devoted enthusiasts kept the art alive,, and today there are a growing number of falconers and falconry clubs. Falconry is completely different from any other field sport. No one who has seen a wild hawk in flight could fail to be attracted by the idea of mastering this ancient art. The modern falconer needs to acquire a variety of different skills: immense patience and a sensitivity to his birds' moods and well-being; a knowledge of field craft and the countryside; leatherwork for repairing and making the furniture required to keep a hawk; an ability to skin and butcher fresh food for the hawks; and a knowledge of game and other wildlife. There is an infinite variety of different types of hawking: game-hawking after pheasant, grouse, partridge and wildfowl; rook-, gull- and magpie-hawking; hedge-hunting and rough-hawking. There are also many different breeds of hawk: long-wings – kestrels, merlins, lugger, peregrine, saker falcons and gyrfalcons, the largest and fastest of them all; short-wings – sparrowhawks and deadly goshawks; broad-wings – assorted buzzards, American Harris hawks and eagles. It is illegal to catch or take the eggs of any wild hawk in this country, and all hawks are aviary-bred.

For our crow-hawking expedition, Terry would be using one of the long-wing hybrid crosses, a peregrine saker-cross or possibly one of the bigger saker gyrfalcons, or gyrfalcon peregrine-crosses. The wide open unfenced land of the Denbigh Moors is ideal country for crow falconry,, with little cover for the crows to flee to and masses of room for the hawk to manoeuvre in. We had lunch with Terry on the outskirts of Denbigh. Afterwards Clarissa and I were photographed holding an enormous hawk owl and a Harris hawk on our gloved wrists. Harris hawks are used largely for rabbiting, but I was interested to see that one was used at Wimbledon this year to scare pigeons away from the tennis courts. Hawks are used with varying success to keep birds off runways and seagulls away from rubbish tips. The problem is that animals in the wild are used to predation. How often have you seen wildlife films where lions or jackals are eating an antelope or zebra, with the rest of the herd grazing peacefully nearby? Birds very quickly return to the area that the hawk is trying to remove them from. On our way back Terry saw an abandoned fledgling magpie, crouching pathetically at the side of a stream.

'I know someone who will hand-rear this,' he said, gently picking it up.

Sticking firmly to main roads, I drove slowly back towards Llanarmon. Between Ruthin and Llangollen, where the road winds its way along the side of a steep gorge, we noticed a huge pile of slag on the side of a mountain.

'Bloody mess,' said Clarissa. 'Wonder what it is?'

'Slate probably,' I hazarded.

A little farther on, while we were negotiating the Horseshoe Pass, Clarissa suddenly announced, 'Look, a sign for a slate mine.'

The sign read: 'Berwyn Slate Quarry Ltd. No Unauthorized Access.'

'Drive in,' shouted Clarissa.

'Can't you read?' I said.

'That doesn't mean us. I want to see a slate mine.'

Well, you don't argue.

I drove in.

Johnny is so much more well-behaved than I am and it took a great deal of persuasion, interspersed with accusations of cowardice, to get him to drive past the 'No Unauthorized Access' sign. I think the winning argument was, 'Well, get out of my car and wait here while I go up'. A long wait amidst waste slate is not, I admit, appealing.

So Johnny, braving his vertigo, drove along the appalling road which was liberally scattered with no-entry signs and we found, at the end, what was clearly a working quarry. A great saw sliced a block of slate with infinite slowness and a noise like chalk screeching across a blackboard. The quarry had clearly been here a long time: there were the ruins of slate-built dwelling houses as we came up. There was also a modern-looking wooden cottage and a caravan. A man appeared and questioned us suspiciously as to our business, then led us into the caravan to meet his wife who, thankfully, recognized me. We had, after all, driven past a lot of no-entry signs! God had again looked after us. It was exactly what we wanted.

Vivian and Mary Bickford had built up a thriving construction business in South Wales which they had handed over to their son. Looking for a project to keep them occupied, they had bought the quarry and were busy revitalizing it. The quarry was started in 1700, and the buildings we had seen had been two-storey dwellings, which they now have permission to restore. Mary took

A backdrop of 'wide ladies'

us up to the quarry itself: it is all above ground, and great towering sheets of slate loomed above us. Perfect! The slate at this quarry was not hard enough for roofing slates, so it provided slate for kitchen surfaces and, where the slate was parti-coloured by the presence of iron oxide, crazy paving. The jagged rock faces resembled a lunar landscape, and there were stunning views over the rural valleys below. What we had found by chance was probably the only small, above-surface slate mine left! The enthusiasm of the owners was a wonderful thing; having worked all their lives to establish themselves, they were now totally caught up in the excitement of restoring an industrial site, not as a Visitor Centre, but for the purpose for which it was created.

Slate is a curious rock. It slices into thin sheets which can be used for all sorts of purposes, the most common of which is roofing tiles. The Welsh slate industry came into its own in the late seventeenth century, providing roofs for the new buildings that the Industrial Revolution made necessary. At its height, it provided half a million tons of tiles a year produced from five million tons of slate. The wastage was horrendous and the great slag-heaps of Bethesda and Blaenau Ffestiniog polluted the landscape just as the coal mines, which came later, did. The mining was mostly underground and, at Blaenau, you can see the vast rock faces that the miners climbed, on flimsy ladders, to place their explosive charges and bring down the sheets.

An underground mine is a frightening and sinister place. The sheets were named by size and thickness, using aristocratic terms: there was a Duchess, a Countess and so forth, finishing with a Wide Lady! The slate was then transported via the canal system to the building sites of the country and, at our mine, we saw where the slate was lowered several hundred feet down to the canal below. We were given a Cook's tour around the plant, with saws and planes all the right size for filming. We drove away happily, with the roof down, and Johnny was even moved to light a cigar!

While we were at the slate mine I noticed that there was quite a lot of heather up there. Mary said that when they first arrived there had been grouse, but there were very few now. She had noticed how the bracken was spreading through the heather, and there seemed to be many more carrion crows. Johnny had always been anxious that we should film grouse-shooting in Wales. I, who knew nothing of the story of the Welsh moors, soon came to see why. Between the wars, the Welsh grouse moors were the *crème de la crème*, bursting with birds. The best shots of the day clamoured to shoot them. Then disaster struck: in one year one of the Flint moors dropped from 300 brace to 43 brace, a pattern that was repeated all over Wales. Everyone is very cagey when you ask them what happened. Bob Williams, a keeper for fifty years in Flint and Denbigh, shook his head sadly and said, 'It was all down to human error.' So exactly what happened?

The red grouse is a wild bird that lives on the heather moors. It feeds almost exclusively on heather shoots and the chicks, after a few early days eating insects, move swiftly on to heather shoots. Heather (*Erica vulgaris*) is a useful plant and where it grows naturally it has provided man with many things: housing, the old Highland black houses had a framework of woven heather stems plastered over with dung; bedding, heather is most comfortable to lie on; dye for clothing, heather produces a bright yellow dye; drink, young heather shoots were used instead of hops in beer; and a pipe to smoke can be carved from the roots. It is, however, a plant that requires ample rainfall and well-drained land as it doesn't like wet feet. The upland moors suit it very well. The grasses of the moors did not provide sufficient grazing for the hill sheep that the graziers of the eighteenth century hefted onto the hill, so the heather was nurtured and its area of growth extended. As the areas of heather moor expanded so did the grouse population.

Grouse has long been an important bird. The phrase 'the glorious twelfth' is rightly associated with the day the grouse season begins, but have you ever asked yourself why no other game season is similarly hailed? The phrase actually refers far more to the fact that it was the date on which the Parliamentary vacation started, and has done since 1531. You can just picture poor

Neglected grouse moor

old Henry VIII sitting gloomily in the Palace of Eltham thinking, 'How can I shut these dreary politicians up and go hawking?' Enlightenment strikes: 'Gadzooks, I will fix the date of the vacation,' and so he passes an edict that the vacation should start on the day on which the grouse season begins. There have been many heated debates in Parliament to set the date of the grouse-shooting season: it is important to find a time after the birds can fly properly and are mature, and before the finish of the harvest releases potential poachers from their husbandry. The Parliament of 1803 heard argument that the sportsmen should be given at least a fortnight's clear grace over the poachers! In Ireland grouse-shooting started on a later date.

Traditionally grouse were walked up behind pointers or spaniels, an exhausting exercise in the heat of an August day wearing thick tweeds and stockings against the heather spikes. Thorn-proof tweed is a 23 oz material. It is virtually waterproof and, being wool, becomes heavier and warmer when wet. It is very durable and lasts for many years, passing from one generation to the next. Today's newly rich prefer a lighter weave, as this distresses and loses its newness more quickly, but they will pay the price in warmth and comfort. Walking through heather is tiring at the best of times, let alone when carrying a gamebag, cartridge belt and shotgun. I have done this and I am talking from painful experience.

A heather moor in full bloom is an exquisite sight, a chequer-board of purple and light green, but the pollen is everywhere and on a hot day the dogs can lose the scent of the birds because of it. The growth of the shotgun, Queen Victoria's passion for Scotland and the Victorian love of shooting have all led to the expansion of grouse-shooting. The first driven grouse were shot at Glenturret Moor, the highest moor in Scotland, in 1861. Shooting a driven grouse is one of the most exciting of sporting pursuits. Shooting at them, which is all I have ever managed, is exciting enough. The grouse come over the brow of a hill at eighty miles an hour, clipping the tops of the heather with the usually lowering skyline leaving the guns with very little visibility. Blink and they've gone over you. The guns stand in butts made of timber and clad with brushwood so that they look as natural as possible to the grouse. A loader will present the second shotgun and make deprecating grunts at your performance, while an adoring female, perched on a shooting stick – not in my case of course – watches your every miss.

When I was young, London, at the end of July, was full of impoverished older men who had been fine shots in their youth – and who had just received a much-prized invitation to shoot on some great estate – bustling about comparing invitations, having their tweeds repaired and getting their shotguns out of pawn. Those days are gone now, there are fewer grouse and taxation has made the great estates commercial. A day's driven grouse shooting costs £1,000 on a good moor. It is largely foreign money, and as one keeper said to me, 'You can get a good day's extra shooting off the birds they miss.'

However, none of this is of any relevance to the decline of grouse on the Welsh moors. So let us examine the situation. The grouse population of the British Isles fell by 82% between 1911 and 1980, and Wales was the worst-hit area. Setting aside the amount of heather that was ploughed up for pasture, and even arable crops, during the Second World War at the instruction of the Government, various reasons suggest themselves. Everyone blames louping-ill, a disease carried to the grouse by a tick, and which can destroy over 50% of grouse chicks in a bad year. Because the ticks also live on sheep, the sheep are blamed but, as one farmer pointed out, the sheep are dipped regularly and this kills thousands of the ticks which are carried off the hill by the sheep.

Johnny, and others, argue that the sheep are an asset on the heather, keeping the plants down to a level where the young grouse can reach the shoots they live on (unchecked heather will grow to three feet in height), and knocking insects off the plants by their passage through the heather so that they become more easily accessible to the very young chicks. On moors where the sheep have been taken off, at the advice of smart London factoring companies, the grouse population has dropped alarmingly. The ticks breed in the bracken, which if it is not sprayed, or rooted out by pigs, will take hold and spread furiously. But the grouse cannot feed on bracken, and bracken kills the heather and so the ticks spread.

However, the grouse, the tick and the heather and the bracken coexisted happily as long as there were well-keepered moors which kept the vermin in check. The planting of extensive forestry since the Second World War has not only reduced the areas of heather, but has also provided a haven for foxes who take the grouse eggs and prey on the chicks. The dealings of some bird protection societies, who seem obsessed with saving raptors to the exclusion of all else (when did you last hear a dawn chorus?), are greatly to blame. In order to prove the real and dangerous effect of raptors to them, the Duke of Buccleuch, a man respected for the husbandry of his estates, gave the RSPB a grouse moor at Langholm in the Scottish Borders. This was a well-keepered moor with plenty of grouse. Within five years there was not one single grouse and the raptor population, which had exploded, was rapidly declining due to a shortage of food. People in towns simply do not understand that a balance must be kept and man must keep it. Perhaps, in this irreligious age, it smacks too much of Genesis!

The Welsh have a further problem. Because of their ancient rights of turbary they have common grazing on the moors. When a misdirected government offered headage payments on sheep (farmers were paid a subsidy per head of sheep they grazed), the farmers crammed the moors with sheep and over-grazed them. As these were not hefted hill sheep, they did not rake up and down the hill: they simply ate out the best. The 30% drop in the grouse population on the Welsh moors between 1950 and 1980 is, in the main, directly traceable to over-grazing. But that still leaves another 50%. The Welsh grouse moors are a perfect example of how man (to use Johnny's words) can antagonize nature, and the cost of getting it wrong. The ploughing of heather during the Second World War did not help, however most heather moor is not suitable for arable farming. The greatest damage is due to mismanagement, removal of sheep entirely, non-spraying of bracken and predators. The hugely reduced population of the other ground-nesting birds who do not feed directly on the heather, and are not affected by louping-ill, especially in the area around the forestry, shows clearly that predators, especially foxes and crows, are to blame. The red grouse may be redeemable, the black grouse possibly, but when a keeper of fifty years' standing like Bob Williams says enthusiastically, 'I saw *a* lapwing', when I see so many on the well-keepered moors of East Lothian, I know that I am staring into the abyss of urban ignorance and want to go away and weep.

There is wistful talk about the return of the black grouse and the curlew and plover, but without the familiar cry of 'goback, goback' – which signals the presence of the red grouse – on the Welsh moors, there will be no shooting value in the moors and, with no value in sheep, there will be no keepering and the bracken and the matt grass will destroy the heather. The guns with their valuable foreign spending power will come no more to the area and even the ramblers who bring sandwiches, tents and camper vans anyway, and are not much of a monetary boost, will be bored by the absence of wildlife other than vermin. The area's economy will decline so that even Mr Blair's theme-park ideas will fail.

Gripped by these gloomy thoughts, and full of admiration for the staunch efforts of our new friends to reverse the terrible decline in the numbers of grouse, we drove home.

CHAPTER NINE

SNIPE PUDDING AND EEL PIE

So strange to be going back to Ireland again. The last time I caught the Holyhead – Dublin ferry I was going the other way, returning from a holiday on the Dingle Peninsula with my father's anaesthetist and his wife and their son Richard. I suppose I was about eleven and had gone first to some cousins in Donegal. Even at that age I remember the food: the appallingly badly cooked lamb and the wonderful unpasteurized milk that I carried in a churn from the farm in Donegal, the mackerel we caught, and the crabs I grubbed from under stones on the beach. I cooked the crabs in tin buckets full of salt water, and the fish over driftwood fires: it was my first attempt at cooking, I suppose.

The shop in the village was also a shebeen run by an old man called O'Cohen, who wore a greasy black bowler. It was dark and full of shadowy figures drinking in the back. I remember the buckets of drinking water I helped carry from the pump at the top of the hill each day; the smell of peat smoke always brings it back. I went on a train on my own to Dingle. I remember perfectly cooked salmon, with home-made mayonnaise which surprised me: it was so unlike the indifferent train food in England. I remember staying with the Morrises, who ate superlatively well, and going salmon fishing for the first time. I caught a little parr which I had to put back, much to my disgust. I had imagined it mounted on a plaque with my name and the date below it. This early disappointment, the midges and the discomfort of trudging through peat-hags quite put me off fishing for years.

I have spent many happy times in the South of Ireland and, being entitled to a passport, can identify with the charm, the blarney and the craik. It is the land where *mañana* doesn't have the same degree of urgency as it does in Spain. The land which produced my grandmother, who wrote to my father on his engagement to my Catholic mother: 'I had rather she were a black heathen whore', which letter my eighteen-year-old mother had framed and hung in the downstairs loo! We were not, however, staying in the South. We were to film in the North because the BBC remit only covers the North: to film in the South is to film abroad. I am a Catholic and the 'Black North' is not a place I choose to go. I had happy enough times there – a childhood boyfriend was half-brother to the Earl of Erne at Crom Castle in County Fermanagh and I enjoyed playing on the massive roofs and going on the Lough in a speedboat – but that does not allay the adult fear of a country torn by religion, particularly when mine is the unpopular one.

It was Johnny's first trip to Ireland and I wished we could have stayed longer in the South, but time was short and we had to press on. The ferry crossing was calm and uneventful. At Drogheda, where my father's family come from, we tried to find somewhere to eat, but it was full of fast-food joints and Tex-Mex eateries, so we went on to Dundalk, where we found a traditional Irish lounge restaurant. This is a peculiarly Irish syndrome where you have a bar full of men and attached to it a lounge bar where women may go and a restaurant. I ordered ham, because you can trust the ham in Ireland, and a large hunk of delicious gammon arrived with potatoes cooked as only the Irish can cook them: so that they taste of potato. On we went, over the open border – marked by a solitary police car – and where once the process took an hour; the only indication that we had arrived in the North was that the road signs measured the distances in miles, not kilometres.

The Adair Arms at Ballymena is the sort of hotel that proliferated in my childhood: long corridors, no lift, overheated but quite comfortable. I am quite certain that had I arrived with a strange man and looked for a double room, I would have been asked to show my marriage lines, as used to be the norm in such places. The hotel's glory was its staff who were endlessly helpful, full of humour and tolerant of the quirks of the most faddish of foreign tourists. Whilst Johnny was on the phone talking to the British Association for Shooting and Conservation, I wandered down to the lobby to chat to the receptionist. I discovered that two schools had been burnt down that night, one in Ballymena itself and the other nearby. In a country that regards education as almost more important than life itself, this was not a good sign. And it made me wonder about the long-term success of the peace process.

When I am in the North I'm always circumspect about mentioning that I'm a Catholic but, with my Ascendancy vowels, if I get it right it can be very productive. This was one of those occasions. I told the young woman on the desk the story of my grandmother's letter and some while later (the Irish are as patient as the Arabs), she told me about Father Kennedy and the Fishermen's Eel Co-operative on Lough Neagh. I rang and was finally put through to a man who proved to be one of those rare souls who is as stubborn and difficult as I am myself. I love it when this happens: it is so rare that one finds a worthy opponent. We sparred for a bit and whilst the good Father made it quite clear that he had no desire to film with the BBC, he grudgingly agreed to see us at 4.15 that afternoon.

Johnny in the meantime had contacted Ronan Gorman and we set off to see him in BASC's offices in Galgorm Castle courtyard. Ronan proved to be the best type of Irish hunk, and I happily imagined him playing football – a game at which he excelled – in those lovely little Gaelic football shorts. As is so often the case with such latter-day Cuchulains, he was also extremely clever and imaginative, and proved to be the guiding hand behind the Lough Beg wetlands development and the purchase of the shooting rights around Lough Beg for BASC.

The land around Lough Beg was the site of the first Protestant settlement in Northern Ireland. James VI, and I, sold the area to the City Livery Companies for a substantial sum of money in a scheme known as the Plantation. Remember we are not talking about the Dark Ages, but the first decade of the seventeenth century. The Livery Companies settled the area and captured the city of Derry, which explains a mystery that has long puzzled me: why Protestants call Derry Londonderry. The reference is, obviously, to the London Livery Companies' capture of the city.

The floor of Lough Beg was given by Charles II to an ancestor of Richard Mulholland, the present owner of Ballyscullion Park. This affected the shooting rights on the foreshore and purlieus of the Lough, as well as on the Lough itself, as it has receded since its seventeenth-century gift. Lough Beg is an important wetland site. It is extremely shallow, a small lough at the north-west corner of the vast Lough Neagh, formed by a broadening of the River Bann. There are several hundred acres of wet grasslands, known as the Strand, which have never been agriculturally developed and consequently support a huge diversity of plant species, many of which are very rare and have magic names like the orchid, 'Irish Lady's Tresses', or the wort, 'Awlwort'.

There is also a massive amount of wildfowl. It is one of the largest European sites for shovelers and pochards and the whooper swans, recalling Yeats's wild swans at Coole (Coole Park is forty minutes' drive away). In summer the grasslands support the largest conglomeration of breeding snipe in Ireland. Lough Beg has been declared a Nature Reserve and a Special Protection Area not only in the British Isles, but also by the European authorities, which means it supports over 1% of several given species in Europe.

As I sit here writing I have beside me an unusual document. It is a copy of an address given on

4 August 1999 by Tony Laws, Deputy Chief Executive of BASC, and Secretary of the Wildlife Habitat Charitable Trust. It describes the links between shooting and conservation which led to the purchase of shooting rights to Ballyscullion, Lough Beg, and the flyway project they have set up in Northern Ireland with Lake Engure. All migrating birds follow flight patterns which are genetically programmed. It is easy for conservationists to follow these paths and make provision for the birds' safety where they pause on their journey, if those stopovers are in a civilized country. Lake Engure is in Latvia and it is the summer breeding ground for many of the wildfowl from Lough Beg.

The dichotomy that lies at the heart of the urban – country divide, it seems to me, is that the urbanites don't seem to realize that the hunter loves and cherishes his prey. The Green Movement calls out for standing headlands, hedgerows, beetle banks and foot-wide verges for fields of arable crops. But that is something that the countryman who shoots or hunts will do willingly to preserve wild game. On Lough Beg the Royal Society for the Protection of Birds and BASC provide sanctuaries which, in addition to being no shooting, should not be walked, cycled or picnicked over in the breeding season. In Northern Ireland – which is so divided by sectarian and religious differences – the RSPB works hand- in- hand with BASC, and recognizes the shooting community's role in conservation. Whereas in England and Scotland, where such divisions are supposed not to exist, the RSPB eschews the shooting community, rendering vast areas of land into wildlife deserts patrolled by predators.

ABOVE: A glorious spot on upper Lough Erne
LEFT: Wildfowl on Lough Beg

BASC have been unbelievably helpful during the making of this programme and I can't thank Ronan Gorman on Lough Beg enough for his help. After a quick and very good lunch in the Castle, a restaurant in the castle that is owned by Christopher Brooke, the owner of Galgorm Castle, Ronan took us out onto the Lough Beg wetlands. It was a beautiful day and I was very happy to stay sitting in my Saab convertible with the roof down, looking out over Church Island, and watching Johnny and Ronan stride off happily to look for snipe.

Church Island, or Inish Toide, to give it its Irish name, is mentioned as a parish in the Annals of Inishfallen as early as 1129. It was ravaged by the Vikings who brought their longboats up the river. It served as the parish church for 1,300 souls until the Plantation, when it was destroyed. It was undoubtedly a centre of clandestine Catholic worship during the Penal times (when practising Catholics were persecuted by the ruling Protestants), and was used as a graveyard until quite recently. On the first Sunday in September it hosts an event which I am keen to film: a Catholic procession across the marshes, with priests in vestments and all the trimmings, followed by Mass and then a picnic and tidy-up of the graves. It is the last example of this ritual of grave-blessing left in the British Isles.

The church boasts a spire because the Earl of Bristol – the Protestant Bishop of Derry, Bishop

Hervey – had it built to improve the view from his house at Ballyscullion. It was the model for Ickworth in East Anglia. Bishop Hervey was a man of exquisite taste and appalling morals, like all his family. The deeply learned and respectable young woman at the restored Bawn (a fortified building which has played a large part in the defences of the area) conceded that he had lady friends, but ducked the issue of his bisexuality with consummate practice. The Bawn has been finely restored, largely due to the fact that the village is the birthplace of Seamus Heaney, the Nobel Prize-winning poet.

Sitting in my car in the sunshine I suddenly realized we were not going to make Father Kennedy's afternoon deadline. I phoned him and was met with an irascible response. He had, as he pointed out with terrible logic, given me a slot and I had failed to make it. He was uninterested in the BBC, the domestic restaurant market or indeed anything I had to offer. But by now I had learnt more about the project and was determined at least to visit it. I played my trump card and informed Father Kennedy that, despite my accent, I am a Catholic. His guard wavered slightly and I managed to get an appointment for 10.15 the following morning. I watched Johnny and Ronan bouncing back though the marshes with a light heart. I too had had my success of the day.

Father Kennedy's baby is the Lough Neagh Eel Fishermen's Co-operative. The Lough, which is more of an inland sea, is the largest source of wild brown eels in Europe. All eels, it is believed, spawn in the Sargasso Sea which is a strange, rather sinister place, full of huge floating rafts of weeds. The Sargasso Sea is in the horse latitudes, so-called because becalmed ships had to throw their dead horses overboard. The area is also known as the Doldrums or, more recently, the Bermuda Triangle and it is no place to be becalmed, believe me. I was becalmed there once and we hove to and hoisted one of the rafts of weeds up by the sixty-foot mainmast, but even then only just over half of it was out of the water. It was made up of layers of reed with different creatures living at different depths. Here, in these reed-rafts, the eels spawn and then great swarms of elvers leave the safety of the reeds and set forth to travel all the way back to the very same spot – which could be anywhere in the world – that their parents left to spawn them in the Caribbean in the first place. The elvers live and grow for fourteen years before returning to the Caribbean as fully grown eels to spawn elvers of their own. Before the eels set off on their return to the Caribbean they close down their digestive tracts and change colour from brown to silver. They are trapped in the autumn and sold as silver eels. The Dutch and German markets particularly crave these large eels. It seems to me that as they are off to spawn, perhaps they should be allowed to get on with it, but there are plenty of eels, so market forces still dictate.

Father Kennedy's story is a triumph for modern Ireland, and I hope someday someone will write up all the missing pieces in the jigsaw. But, briefly, Charles II gave the fishing on Lough Neagh to his friend, the Marquis of Donegal, and for centuries he ran an eel monopoly. At the beginning of the nineteenth century a Lord Donegal formed a partnership with a Dutch consortium to ship eels to Holland for smoking. All eels had to be sold to the company, which dictated the price.

The east side of the Lough was industrial and Protestant, while the west side was largely Catholic, and the fishermen were of original Irish descent. In the 1960s things began to change, as pressure grew to increase Catholic rights and interests. Consequently, as parish priest for the area, Father Kennedy obtained a release from parish duties and was able to set up a fishermen's co-operative and change the status quo. Today the Co-operative has bought out the Dutch company and controls all the eel-fishing on Lough Neagh. Exactly how this was achieved remains as secret as the location of Cuchulain's grave.

Johnny and I arrived at the eel fishery promptly at 10.10 am. There was nothing to see but some huge fishing traps, on which perched perhaps a dozen herons waiting expectantly. The Co-operative building is large, fine and modern with some excellent ironwork of eels: obviously money has not been spared in its construction. We went inside and were kept waiting with nowhere to sit for some little while before we were ushered into Father Kennedy's office. The good Father is a thickset man with a bullet-shaped head and a stubborn jaw. We sat and listened as he told us that the Co-operative shipped 5,000 tons of eels to Holland and Germany each year, and that there were one hundred fishermen in the Co-operative whose catch was collected by the fishery trucks in numbered containers. The catch is then weighed and the amount credited to each fisherman's account. The eels are packed on ice and shipped, live, to the Continent as freight, on passenger flights, and arrive at the smokeries, or the fishmongers', within twenty-four hours. Time is of the essence because the Dutch want their eels live. A small amount is shipped to Billingsgate.

Eel traps on Lough Neagh

167

Father Kennedy, it emerged, had had a lot of his time wasted by television companies in the past and was not interested in us. I wheedled, cajoled and flattered, all to no avail. However, I guessed that the strong pound must be hurting them and pointed out that the smokeries on the Cumbrian coast were crying out for eels. He riposted that eels were bred in Scotland. I replied that the ones in Lough Neagh were wild. Maybe that did the trick, or maybe it was our obvious interest, or maybe God intervened, but Father Kennedy relented and took us through to the packing plant. I told Father Kennedy that it was a real pleasure to meet someone as stubborn as myself, which nearly got a laugh out of him and certainly merited a splutter!

The sorting and packing building is a vast and splendidly built rectangular brick hall, with high ceilings and good floors. A lot of money has been spent to produce it. Along either side run a series of tanks for keeping the eels alive. One of these tanks was full of eels which had been brought in the night before. Pressure jets kept the water aerated and moving and, although the eels were soporific when we touched them, they were alive. The tanks on the far wall, which stood empty, were for the winter's silver eel harvest and Father Kennedy pointed out that they could be salinated where necessary. A series of wooden troughs ran from the entrance, and two huge sets of scales separated the troughs from a very large table. About a dozen men lined the troughs and table.

A small truck had drawn up as we arrived carrying about twenty metal containers, each the

The silent eel selectors

size of an average kitchen sink and marked with a number. Each container was tipped onto the first trough and the eels that were too small were sorted by hand into a drain that led back into the trough. The eels were then channelled down the trough by means of hand-held wooden scrapers. The eels were very active, squirming their way along the trough in a sinuous mass. (Eels travel miles across country to find water if their home dries up. They are very good movers on land, as long as there is some moisture: on their land migrations dew or rain is quite sufficient.)

These eels were a brawny yellow colour with here or there one that was already turning silver, although it was still early in the season. Once any undersized eels had been returned to the Lough, the eels were channelled into a basket which was carried across by hand to the scales and weighed, and the weight recorded by a clerk onto the main ledger against the fisherman's name and number. The basket was then tipped onto a table where any large eels were picked out with tongs and set aside for specialist customers. The remaining eels were channelled down the table with the same hand-held scrapers and into bags which, in turn, were laid in cardboard boxes carrying the Co-operative's logo, packed with ice bags and sealed with plastic tape for shipment to the Continent. The men worked in total silence so that it was a very surreal scene with the noiseless movement of the eels, the echoing hall and the mute men. Each container was dealt with separately so that there could be no confusion between catches.

Dr Moriarty, in his definitive work on eels, written in 1972, dealt not only with the life cycle of the eel, but also confirmed as true many of the supposed myths attached to them. There are indeed eel balls: large knots of eels intertwined for an unknown reason, which live and grow in this state. A dowager Duchess of Hamilton, living in the early eighteenth century, confirmed the fact that eels will travel quite some distance across dry land to feast on green peas, of which they are very fond. They break open the pods, making a strange smacking noise with their lips, before consuming the peas and returning to their ponds. Dr Moriarty also confirmed that eels will make quite long journeys across dry land, either travelling through the dew or following the drainage system, to find new habitats if their old one has drained or dried out.

Men have always caught eels and there are many ways to do this. Ingenious eel traps are installed in rivers, or at the entrances to mill-races. Huge-bladed eel spears are used for fishing by night with torches (the eels come up to the light) or, as on Lough Neagh, eels are caught in drift-nets or with hand lines. Eels are very rich in fat which makes them ideal for smoking, and the local fishermen simply skin them, throw them into a frying-pan and allow them to cook in their own fat. Personally I like them stewed. To skin an eel you nail its head to a plank, cut round the neck and pull the skin off in one piece.

On our way to Enniskillen I drove Johnny down the 'marching streets' which exist in every town or village. I have never seen so many Union Jacks in the Orange areas, nor so many Irish flags in the Catholic ones. Silhouettes of gunmen in Balaclavas, and of RUC Officers with blacked-out faces, adorned the walls. The air was thick with menace. At one point, when we asked for directions, we were told to turn left past the police station. Johnny was truly aghast when he saw his first Ulster police station. They are built like small forts with high, thick windowless walls, their outer walls frilled with barbed wire and decorated with security cameras. The metal door is as thick as one in any Norman castle. A Northern Irish police station brings home more quickly than anything else the nature of the Province. When I was a child they were always blowing up the Enniskillen police station and I could never imagine how. Riverdance has more chance of uniting Ireland than the English Parliament, but I truly hope I may have to eat those words.

Rural Ulster is like the England of our childhood with its small fields and the hay fever I thought had gone with age returned with a vengeance, in response to all the seeding grasses. I was amazed to discover that it was English agriculture that had changed, and not my allergies. With the roof down, and sneezing intermittently, we rolled on to Enniskillen.

One of the reasons for coming to Northern Ireland was to film snipe-shooting. We went to Ballanaleck on the shore of Upper Lough Erne, which is part of the vast area that the Lough Erne Wildfowlers Council manage, in association with BASC, for the Department of Agriculture. The LEWC was formed in 1991 and is made up of eleven wildfowling clubs representing the greatest majority of shooting sportsmen in County Fermanagh.

Upper and Lower Lough Erne, which make up the Erne Lakeland, form one of the most extensive waterway systems in Western Europe. The two are joined by a network of channels and small loughs which are all part of the Erne River. The scenery is spectacularly beautiful with heavily wooded shorelines punctuated with water-meadows, where cattle graze knee-deep in buttercups. Lower Lough Erne is a vast lough: five miles across and, in places, seventy feet deep. Upper Lough Erne is an enchanting jumble of little wooded islands covered in willows, oak and ash. The area is steeped in antiquity, with many ruins of early Christian settlements, and it is a part of the world that Clarissa knew from childhood holidays staying at Crom Castle.

Like so much of Ireland, the Ernes are a paradise for wildfowl, both resident and migratory. Many species that have become rare in the rest of Britain live in this natural habitat. There are great-crested grebes, water rail, different varieties of sandpiper, whooper swans and, among the reeds and rushes, lovely little grasshopper warblers. There is a profusion of mallard, teal, widgeon and, of particular interest to us, snipe. Snipe-shooting in Ireland has the same fabled ring to it that their hunting has, and for much the same reason. The countryside has not been eroded by monoculture, as it has on the British mainland. I had remarked to Clarissa, once we were free of Dublin and heading north towards the mountains of Mourne, that the countryside reminded me of somewhere I had been to, but couldn't quite remember. Then it came back to me. All the little fields, with their profusion of wild flowers and birdlife, were the landscape of my childhood.

This is what it used to be like before the bulldozers and drainage machines got to work flattening the hedgerows and creating great ugly, featureless fields where nothing grows but grain and the habitat and food source of our wildlife is destroyed by pesticides. God, when I think what scientists, and the Ministry of Agriculture, have done to this green and pleasant land.

Wildlife thrives in Ireland because conservationists have learnt from the appalling mistakes that have been made in other parts of these islands. The population is still predominantly rural and, as a result, precious values and traditions have been preserved. Conservationist bodies, like the RSPB, are run by reasonable people with country backgrounds and connections, who appreciate the vital role that field sports play in the management of wildlife. There are swarms of snipe in Ireland because their wetland habitat has not been drained, as part of agricultural improvements, in the same way that has happened in most of the rest of the British Isles.

Snipe are extraordinary little birds. They weigh not much more than 6 oz, and the smaller jacksnipe weighs half that. In my part of the world we call them heather-bleaters, because of the weird and lovely sound they create when they dive from a great height, with their outer tail-feathers spread. To many a hill farmer this eerie sound, on a moonlit March night, is the first indication of approaching spring.

A snipe's long narrow bill is almost one-third of its total body length and has, at the end of it, a highly sensitive tip which enables it to sense worms below the surface before it starts to probe

Pudding potential

for them. They are present all year round in Ireland, but huge numbers start to migrate south from Scandinavia in late September and October, as soon as the ground there becomes too hard. They return home in March. The great attraction of snipe is their delicious eating and that of all game-birds, they are the most unpredictable and difficult to shoot.

The movement of snipe is generally governed by laws about which we know little or nothing. In one season they will be numerous at a certain marsh. The next year perhaps not one will visit the same spot. On one day there will be wisps of them all over a locality, but a night of frost

Snipe shooting

will drive them away, while a change of wind will bring them back again. Because of the soft pulpy membrane at the end of their bill, everything is weather-dependent. If severe weather sets in they will disappear altogether, perhaps migrating further south or to some warm salt marsh near the sea.

There is something unique about shooting snipe. Such a volume of inconclusive advice and the predictability of good or bad sport, so completely different from any other, that it acquires a perverse charm to which aficionados can easily become addicted. Most people of experience agree that the only rule is to approach the bogs and marshes where you think they may be, downwind. Snipe, like most birds when flushed, will rise against the wind and then hang in the air for a second, facing you before darting away. Snipe and woodcock zigzag violently from side to side, eventually straightening out after a dozen yards or so. They do this to conquer the wind and bring their power of flight under control. This, and the fact that you can never tell at what distance they will rise in front of you – in some weather conditions they lie so tight you can practically tread on them, in others they consistently get up just out of range – make snipe the most difficult and challenging shot of all game-birds.

Ronan Gorman, Director of BASC for Northern Ireland, hearing that we were going to Lough Erne, immediately suggested that we contact Robert Irvine, the Secretary of the Lough Erne Wildfowlers Council – another example of how the network of co-operation works in the countryside. Robert's response to my telephone call was unequivocal and enthusiastic. We met him at Ballanaleck on the shore of Upper Lough Erne.

Like other management schemes operated by wildfowling clubs and BASC in the British Isles, the LEWC have a strict code of conduct for members which insists, among other things, that all wildfowling is carried out under current legislation governing wildfowling practice. Their management aims include ensuring that wildfowling is sustainable on Lough Erne and maintaining and improving sites of nature conservation interest, particularly in relation to waders and wintering wildfowl.

Wardening is one of the most important roles that wildfowlers perform in managing the area, particularly over refuge sites, where there are agreements with conservation bodies that no shooting should take place. Wildfowlers are ideally suited to a policing role as they are out at the same time that irresponsible behaviour – poaching and indiscriminate shooting – is likely to take place. They are able to monitor the numbers and movement of rare species and to control predators. Mink have become a considerable problem in the area and although there are no mink-hounds, I understand that the matter will soon be in hand.

The wildfowling season in Northern Ireland begins on 1 September and runs through until 31 January. The big migratory influx doesn't usually occur until later in October but there would be plenty of resident snipe for our visit in mid-September. Most snipe-shooting is walked up over marshy land and my one caveat for the venture was Clarissa's dicky foot. She is dead game for anything and never lets on, but walking over rough ground is extremely painful.

Lough Erne offers an unusual form of snipe-shooting which solved the problem. Snipe are driven over guns in boats. Two or three boats with an oarsman, one or two guns and a retriever. They move slowly, in line, along the shore in those parts where the Lough narrows, or where there is a series of islands. Every so often the boats stop and the shore party work towards them with dogs, through the reeds on the water's edge. Snipe break across the boats to the land on the other side. It seemed ideal and tremendously challenging. The prospect of the first season's snipe was positively mouth-watering. If we shot enough, Clarissa and I could experiment with a favourite dish of Edward VII: snipe pudding.

Time was getting on when we left Robert and drove to the pretty town of Enniskillen, dominated by the ancient castle, to find a hotel for the night. No sooner had we got there when we realized I had forgotten to take any photographs of the Lough for our publishers and we were forced to retrace our steps.

'Not to worry,' boomed Clarissa. 'I shall telephone the Tourist Board and they can arrange something for us. Find the number and leave the rest to me.'

Instructions fulfilled, I handed her the mobile telephone.

'My name,' she said, enunciating clearly, 'is Clarissa Dickson Wright.' There was a pause. 'You have heard of me I take it? Oh. Well. You will have heard of the television programme *Two Fat Ladies*? You haven't? You must be unique. Seventy million other people have.'

It was difficult to know what to say, so I sat tight and said nothing.

In stony silence we arrived at Daryadd Quay, opposite Inisrath Island, with its magnificent Victorian house which is now occupied by the Hare Krishnas. A lone figure was spinning for pike at the end of the quay and, nearer the shore, someone was tinkering with a sailing boat.

'I shall ask that man if he would mind taking our photograph,' announced Clarissa.

'Better let me do it,' I said, keeping out of arm's reach. 'He might not know who you are.'

As it happened, before either of us could speak to him, the man approached Clarissa and said, with charming old world courtesy, 'Clarissa Dickson Wright I believe? My wife has your acquaintance. Perhaps you would like to have tea with us.' Moments later we were following him at speed, down a series of ever-narrowing lanes.

'I suppose you would like to know who that chap is?' Clarissa asked after a while.

'Go on then,' I said. 'Who is he?'

'I haven't the first clue,' she told me. 'It's possible his wife was at school with me. Lots of people were you know. I just hope he hasn't muddled me up with Jennifer Paterson. It has happened.'

In due course we arrived at a once-magnificent Georgian house with cockerels bickering on the lawn. All was revealed when the mystery woman came down the steps from the front door to greet us. It was Jennifer Hicks, the sister of one of Clarissa's greatest friends. Tea was served in a kitchen filled with piles of sporting periodicals and old copies of *Bailey's Hunting Directory*. Jennifer and Michael's fourteen-year-old granddaughter, an enchanting girl with golden hair and peridot eyes, showed us photographs of the Sunnyland Beagles to whom she is a junior whipper-in. With little persuasion she ran upstairs to fetch her pet ferret, Pickles, from its hutch in her bedroom. From time to time her beautiful mother, with shoulder-length mauve hair, wafted through the kitchen. A small boy and a little girl of African origin came and sat, perfectly mannered, and drank their tea in a corner. At one point the lodger from upstairs joined us, a lady whose occupation was writing the potential bestseller *A Smoker's Guide to Air Travel*.

'Catch the ferret,' said Michael, 'and bring Dungeon in to meet these nice people.'

An incredibly ancient harrier was led in and tottered across to lay his head on my knee.

'Hell of a good hound in his day. He scatters hair and filth all over the house, but we love him dearly. Some people call him Pungent.'

It was a magical afternoon with a timeless quality to it. As we drove away Clarissa turned to me. 'That,' she said, 'is what they call the Irish experience.'

Scarcely changed since Somerville and Ross.

The other reason for visiting Upper Lough Erne was to include an element of coarse fishing in the programme. Coarse fishing is an enormously popular sport which supports a huge fishing tackle and accessory industry. We particularly wanted to try our luck at *Esox lucius* or pike, the ultimate and most thrilling of all coarse fish. Pike earned their Latin name from the Greek word

Spinning for pike on Lough Erne

175

'lukos', meaning wolf. Wolves are the most ravenous and cruel amongst beasts; pike are the most greedy and devouring of fish. I love the idea that our freshwater streams, lakes and ponds, with their gentle bream, dace, grayling, perch, rudd and tench also contain a piscine monster which has scarcely changed from prehistoric times, and whose fossil remains confirm that it has been around for longer than any other freshwater fish in the British Isles.

A pike is the most perfect killing machine, capable of fantastic explosions of speed. Its long, sinuous body and dog-like head are powered forward by a disproportionately large tail, assisted by a dorsal fin that is set unusually far back. Very little that a pike gets hold of escapes. Its monstrous mouth is filled with a staggering collection of teeth. The lower jaw contains a large quantity of incisors for piercing and crushing, which the fish uses to grip and immobilize its prey. The roof of its mouth has several hundred smaller teeth all pointing inwards towards a gullet that is capable of expanding like a snake's, and there is much of the snake about a pike. In 1890 a certain Dr Genzik assured H Cholmondeley-Pennel, Queen Victoria's Inspector of Sea Fisheries, that he had definitely seen European pike that had retractable fangs similar to a viper's. Not only that, but their jaws were able to dislocate just like a python's. Unfortunately he was unable to produce any specimens to support his assurances.

Pike also have the extraordinary ability to alter their wonderful camouflage colouring to suit the location. In clear water the network of spots and blotches covering the body become greeny-

A pike is a fearsome beast

grey, to blend in with the reeds on the shoreline. In peaty water these become brown and yellow, and darker still if bad weather brings down a lot of topsoil into their habitat. They will become the colour of weak milky coffee in floodwater. Pike also have an immensely varied diet. They scavenge for the dead and dying fish lying on the bottom. Equally, they are patient and stealthy hunters who wait in ambush amongst rushes at the water's edges, tree roots protruding from a bank, timbers of a landing stage, or the stanchions of a bridge. A pike will lie still, tail moving imperceptibly just below the surface, its malevolent, unwinking steel-grey eyes searching for an unsuspecting fish to swim within range. When one does, the pike erupts out of hiding. If the prey is small it is gulped down whole, otherwise it is seized lengthways and carried off to some convenient place where the pike can manoeuvre the body round until it is eatable, head first. Generally speaking, like most predators, pike are solitary creatures, but they will hunt in packs and herd a shoal of small fish – the way sheepdogs herd sheep – into some bottleneck before charging amongst them with gaping jaws, whipping the water into a froth as they commit great slaughter.

Pike not only have exceptional eyesight, they also have an acutely sensitive nervous system that enables them to be aware of fish and other prey, even when they cannot see them. Tiny connected ducts which run the entire length of a pike's body detect sound, vibration and changes in physical pressure in the water around them. On the head are more ducts around the eyes, under the chin and lower jaw which do the same thing. And, if all else fails, their sense of smell enables them to pick up a scent easily and follow it up like a hunting hound. As long as there is a food source somewhere in their habitat, a pike can find it under practically any condition.

Nor are they the least bit choosy about what they eat. Smaller pike, up to 20–25 lbs, vary their diet by eating water voles, frogs, toads, newts and crustaceans. After waterfowl have hatched their chicks and are teaching them to swim, many become victims to pike. The larger species grow four feet long and weigh 50 lbs, and there are many records of double that weight. They will attack practically anything, particularly in cold weather when they are hungry: 'The half-frozen dyke that hungers into madness every plunging pike.'

There are accounts of otters, dogs, cattle and even humans being attacked. Dr Genzik, yes, him again, recounts a story of swimming in the Danube with a party of fellow students whilst studying medicine in Vienna, when one screamed and sank. On being rescued and dragged to shore, a 32 lb pike was found clinging to his ankle. Not even Her Majesty's Controller of Fisheries was free from attack. A forty-pounder, which he had assumed to be dead, leapt up and seized H Cholmondeley-Pennel by the upper thigh, inflicting horrid injury and subsequently chewing through the stick used to prise its jaws open. Had he not instinctively turned sideways at the *moment critique* I doubt that he would have written his life's work, *The Sporting Fish of Great Britain*, with quite such enthusiasm.

Tranquillity at the end of a day's fishing

More recently, a Mr Reade of Muckamore, County Antrim, wrote to *The Field* on the subject of a shot pheasant landing in open water in a patch of marsh. It disappeared as two spaniels, sent to retrieve it, reached the spot. Both dogs turned and swam frantically for shore. This letter produced a flood of similar ones from wildfowlers who had lost quarry to pike and one lady who had been badly bitten when she trailed her hand in the water whilst being rowed by her husband across a Scottish loch. Apparently she suffered for months from the bite. Stories like these saved me from the expense of fencing off a pond in the garden when my son was small. Because his mind was filled with tales of the horror that lurked in the deep, he contented himself by hurling stones into it from a safe distance.

Upper Loch Erne was an ideal choice for pike-fishing. There is a mass of reedy cover for the brutes to lie up in, stretches of open water and plenty of deep holes where, hopefully, the big boys would be lurking. Both Upper and Lower Lough Erne have any number of marinas from which one can hire cabin cruisers. Personally I think these aquatic caravans ought to be banned. They are an eyesore in a beautiful place like the Ernes, and do nothing for the peace of mind of the lovely migratory birds and nesting wildfowl with their pollution, litter, noise, bow waves and diesel smoke. Furthermore they contribute enormously to the spread of Zebra mussels. Zebra mussels are highly invasive and, although they only appeared in the Erne water system in 1996, they breed at an incredible rate and are already clinging in great bundles to piers, quays, jetties and, in particular, boats. Their impact on the ecology of the Lough is malignant, and they foul the spawning grounds of fish such as the Arctic char and the pollan.

Robert Irvine had very kindly promised to arrange for a ghillie to take Clarissa and me out in the same type of eighteen-foot boat that we would use for snipe-shooting to fish some of the deep holes with bait for big pike and to troll back and forth for the smaller fish – if you can call twenty-pounders small fish. We also thought we could fulfil Steve's desire for a different slant on fishing by hiring one of the cruisers and trolling off the back of it. Judging by the brochures, some of the horrid things can be quite luxurious, with all the basic essentials – hot water and flushing lavatories – and there was another attraction: Clarissa is a highly competent sailor, having spent much of her time ruling the waves around the Caribbean. The complexities of the Erne Waterway, generally regarded as a navigational nightmare, would be nothing to an old sea-dog of her experience.

For our trolling expeditions we would require a couple of sturdy boat-rods and various other odds and ends: a 20 lb breaking-strain line, and braided wire traces to connect the line to any one of the infinite variety of artificial lures with their treble hooks. We would also need a strong gaff and, presumably, something heavy like a mason's mallet to brain our catch once it had been hauled on board, and before it latched onto something soft. I name no names. The simplest form of trolling is to trail the line behind a boat, preferably one that is being obligingly rowed by someone who enjoys that sort of thing, or has been paid to do it.

Where the bottom shelves and drops away, the rower rows slowly to allow the lure to work deeply. In shallow water, encouraged by shouts of 'faster', and handfuls of cash, the rower flails along to bring the lure up, free of weeds. Revolving quickly through the water, the lure resembles a small fish swimming busily along. Behind the motor-cruiser we would be using heavy spoons, keeping the speed slow enough to stop the spoon surfacing. Over the deeper holes, wherein the leviathans lie, we would be using bait, one of the oldest methods of catching pike. We know something about catching pike from early literature on the subject. In the seventeenth century fishing in general started to become an enormously popular sport. A method of splicing horsehairs together was developed which enabled fishermen to fish further out for the first time. Primitive reels started to appear and, inevitably, enthusiasts couldn't wait to share their views with those who could read. Seizing quills and handfuls of parchment they started to write about the new sport of fishing.

In 1600 the great fishing-book bonanza – which seems to have continued unabated up to the present day – began. Such masterpieces as William Lauson's *Secrets of Angling* appeared in 1620. Lauson had a lot to say about pike bait and recommended, among other suggestions, a paste of powdered mummy, and man's fat. If these failed, 'A young whelpe, kitlin or such like is good bait for a Luce.' Luce was the old word for pike. Thirty years later the scholarly Izaak Walton, in his definitive *Compleat Angler*, offered a refinement: 'Tie fifteen yards of stout cord to a pinioned duck. Tie to the duck a further length of cord with a large hook on the end. Attach hook to an active mature frog. Shoo duck in the direction of pike habitat.'

For our little expeditions we would be using fresh dead bait, something irresistible like a succulent dace or chub, and a much stronger - weighted line, treble hooks with a sliding float on the line set well over depth beneath a stop-knot. The float bobbing would give us an early indication that a pike had grabbed the bait and, according to the locals, was a deadly effective method of catching them.

The other great advantage of being on a cabin cruiser was that we could be seen preparing, cooking and eating the fruits of our efforts. The snipe would need to be plucked and their heads skinned. The brains are a delicacy and, unlike other game-birds, except woodcock, their intestines are not removed and they are cooked with them inside. There is a reason for this: when snipe or woodcock are flushed, they empty the contents of their stomachs. By so doing, their intestines become edible.

Pike are delicious and their firm white flesh has been greatly esteemed for centuries. It featured regularly at banquets. Vanière praises pike in his *Praedicum Rusticum*:

Lo, the rich pike to entertain your guests,

Smokes on the board, and decks a royal feast.

Richard II had pike at the blow-out he put on for William of Wykeham, the celebrated Bishop of Winchester, in 1394, and they were on the menu at the enthronement of George Nevill, Archbishop of York, in 1466. The correct method of carving a pike found its way into the *Boke of Kervynge*, printed by Caxton's successor, Wynkyn de Worde, at the beginning of the sixteenth century. In those days you would chine a salmon, splay a bream, side a haddock and splatt a pike.

The great drawback to cooking and eating pike is the simply incredible number of bones it contains. Most dishes require the meat to be laboriously separated from the bones and reconstituted in some way. Clarissa, however, has a little-known recipe for marinating pike in such a way that the small bones dissolve and, no doubt, amongst her collection of antique cooking equipment, there will be a pike-splatting tool.

CONCLUSION

The cruellest aspect of the political manipulation of the urban and rural divide is the impact it has on our countryside children. When I was a child, stewardship of the countryside was a matter of national pride, and those involved in it had every right to be proud of their achievements. Now our children are made to feel that there is something wrong with what they and their parents have been brought up to love and respect. We are talking about our national heritage. There is no greater crime against humanity than to create an ethnic minority where none has previously existed.

Terry Large, the falconer, told recently of a small boy whose essay on the countryside – in which he described all the glories of nature – won, overwhelmingly, a regional first prize, but he was too ashamed to admit that his father was a gamekeeper.

What we basically hope for is that, through this book, and the television programmes, we will have done something to preserve, for future generations, the opportunity to continue this stewardship as our forebears have done for centuries.

There is another equally important aspect and that is the one of freedom of choice. You don't have to like field sports, but because you don't like, understand or approve of them, why should this give you the right to prevent those who do? Isn't mutual tolerance the mark of a truly democratic society? Where there is no freedom of choice – as we have seen all too clearly in the previous century – horrors result.

And finally, you might like to consider Rousseau's words: 'It is the country which makes the land; it is the country-people who make the nation.'

Go on, what happened then?

GLOSSARY

OF COUNTRY (AND A FEW OTHER) TERMS FOR TOWNIES

Definitions of words used in field sports, that our (Townie) editor suggested we should include in this book.

ANTIS
Rent-a-crowd who oppose field sports and who demonstrate their opposition at events, frequently with abuse and violence and often resorting to illegal means such as spraying hounds with chemicals or injuring horses.

ARGOCAT
A six-wheeled amphibious all-terrain vehicle used specifically for stalking and on grouse moors.

BAG LIMITS
The maximum number of game-birds that may be shot at any one time.

BANK
Nightmarish Irish hunting obstacle. A steeply banked two-sided earth erection often rising to five feet or more. It is necessary for the horse to jump onto the top of the bank, change feet, and jump down the other side. They say, in Ireland, that when approaching a bank you wish you'd been to Mass.

BASC
The British Association for Shooting and Conservation.

BEAT
Riparian ownership of a stretch of river-bank and its fishing.

BEATERS
People engaged to 'beat' through undergrowth, woods, etc., to flush out game towards guns (qv).

BLANK (when hunting)
Empty.

BLUE HARES (and BROWN HARES)
Indigenous hare of the British Isles, except Northern Ireland. A moorland creature, it turns white in winter and is a dark chocolatey brown in summer. The brown hare was introduced to these islands by the Romans for coursing purposes.

BRACE
A pair of game-birds or greyhounds.

BREECH LOADER
Invented in France in 1850. For the first time a gun could be broken and loaded by a cartridge at the breech rather than by the muzzle. It revolutionized game shooting.

BRENT
A goose. A small, dark, reptilian winter visitor to the British Isles from Arctic Russia. It is strictly protected. Numbers are on the increase since the collapse of Communism and the closure of political gulags: guards and prisoners varied their diet by eating the eggs of nesting birds.

BURN
Scottish word for stream.

BUTTS
A concealed stand for grouse-shooting.

CEILIDH
Scottish piss-up with music and reel dancing. Great fun for those who can dance.

CHECK (as in checking hounds)
Hounds hunt entirely by scent. They are said to 'check' when they temporarily lose the scent of their quarry.

CLEUGH
Scottish word for a steep-sided ravine.

CORRIE
Circular sheltered hollow on the hillside, from the Gaelic 'coire' which means kettle or cauldron.

COUNTRY (as in the Hunt country)
The area hunted by a particular pack of hounds.

COUNTRYSIDE ALLIANCE, THE
The new name for the British Field Sports Society which was started in the 1930s. It champions the countryside, country sports and the rural way of life and works closely with other countryside organisations to promote awareness of country issues among the media, the public and politicians.

COUPLE (as in ten couple of hounds)
Hounds are always counted in twos.

COURSING
Where gaze-hounds are used to chase a hare or other animal.

COVERT
Correct term for the woods, gorse or bushes where foxes live.

CRAIK
Animated chat.

CREEL FISHING
Fishing with traps made of wickerwork, particularly used for catching lobsters, prawns, langoustines, etc.

DAME SCHOOL
The place you get sent to before preparatory school. Run by a bossy female.

DEAD STOCK
Most hunt kennels have enough staff to provide a dead-stock recovery service to farmers in their hunting country. The flesh is fed to the hounds.

DEW CLAWS
The non-functional claw, in dogs, at the heel. Often removed to avoid the claw growing into the skin.

DL
Deputy Lieutenant.

DRAFT FOXHOUNDS
To remove a hound from a pack either through age or because it doesn't fit in for some reason – perhaps it is too fast or too slow. A pack of hounds must work together as a team. Drafted hounds go to other packs where they will fit in better; old bitches go for breeding; dog hounds go to a pack with a slower pace, like mink-hounds. The process is similar, and the terminology the same, with flocks of sheep.

DRAW
When hounds are seeking the scent of a fox in a covert (qv).

DRIVEN
The opposite of walking up (qv). Quarry is driven towards guns (qv) by beaters (qv). It evolved with the development of the breech loader (qv).

EARTHS
Foxes live in 'earths'.

ELVERS
Young eels.

ENTERED HOUND
A hound becomes entered when it hunts as part of the pack for the first time.

FACTOR
A land agent who manages an estate for a landlord. Robert Burns called his dog after the factor who ran the estate on which he rented a farm. Need we say more?

FAST SHALLOWS
In a river. Self-explanatory.

FELL-HOUNDS
Specifically bred for hunting in the high fells of the Lake District. They are lighter framed than other hounds and faster. Fell-hunting is done on foot for obvious reasons, and hounds hunt more independently. Hounds need a good nose and must throw their tongues freely. (Townies: this means make a lot of noise.)

FIELD (as in of a Hunt)
The mounted followers on a day's hunting are the field.

FLANKERS
Flanking involves waving a flag at a hare to ensure she comes onto the running ground near the slipper (qv) and keeps straight during the run up. Also used in guiding driven grouse over the butts (qv).

FLESH HOUSE
A building where dead stock (qv) is skinned and butchered.

FLIGHTING
Shooting wildfowl as they flight in to land.

FLUSHED (as in when a bird is)
Driven from cover.

FOLLOWERS
People, other than the field (qv), who follow a hunt.

FOOT ROTTING (lambs)
Fusiformis necrophesus. It is the very smelly softening and decay of sheep's hooves. It has to be removed with a knife.

FORM
The shallow depression in which a hare nests.

FOX LAMPING
Attempting to shoot foxes at night by catching them in the beam of a high-powered light. Limited to land that is accessible to vehicles and out of rifle-shot from houses.

FURNITURE (as in a hawk's leather furniture)
Term used for all the paraphernalia used by a falconer in training and keeping a hawk.

GAFF
Hook on the end of a pole. For bringing a caught fish in to the bank whilst it is still on the line.

GARRON
A Highland pony. I used one for years to get round the sheep.

GAZE-HOUNDS
Those that hunt entirely by sight. Possibly the source of the word greyhound.

GHILLIE
Originally a Scottish chief's personal steward. Now the term is understood to mean the long-suffering soul who looks after one whilst fishing. He guides the fisherman and is sometimes rather taciturn. Also see STALKER.

GIMMER
A young female hill sheep. A ewe lamb becomes a hogg at six months, and a gimmer when shorn for the first time, at thirteen months.

GLIDES
The neck and tail of a slow, deep pool.

GOLDEN HOOF
An expression used to describe the boom in sheep-farming during the eighteenth and nineteenth centuries when sheep spread into the Highlands.

GRALLOCH
The innards of a deer. The art of disembowelment.

GRAVELLY RUNS
Fast-flowing water, deeper than stickles (qv), which runs over pebbles.

GUANO
Goose shit, to the less refined.

GUNS
The correct term for people who shoot, just as rods (qv) is the correct term for people who fish.

HARDY
Famous firm of rod-makers.

HARRIER PACKS
Hounds that hunt hares. Originally they hunted all kinds of game. The hounds are bigger than a beagle and smaller than a foxhound.

HAYES
Saxon form of hunting, similar to tainchel (qv).

HEFTS
An unfenced area of hill land on which a specific number of sheep live.

HILL-HOUNDS
Similar to fell-hounds (qv), but hunted in country which, though hilly, hounds can be ridden to, such as much of Northumberland, and similar country.

HILL TOPPING
An expression used to describe hunting in the Cheviots, the first rule of which is never to come down. Do that and you lose hounds and probably yourself.

HIND
A female red deer.

HOBDAY(ED)
Invented by a man called FT Hobday (1869–1939), it is an operation performed on the larynx of a horse to improve its breathing. It leaves an open hole in the throat which is stopped with a metal plug that can be removed to improve air flow.

HOUNDS SPEAKING
Giving tongue, or, for Townies, making a lot of noise.

HUNT SERVANTS
People who are employed by the Hunt, such as a kennelman or a professional huntsman.

HUNTSMAN
A Hunt Servant who hunts the hounds and is responsible for their welfare.

IFAW
The International Fund for Animal Welfare, an American organization.

JILL (AND HOB)
Female (and male) ferrets.

JP
Justice of the Peace.

KEEPER
Short for gamekeeper: the person who breeds and manages the gamebirds on an estate, controls predators and prevents poaching.

KITLIN
Kitten.

LAMPING
See FOX LAMPING.

LARSEN TRAPS
A cage with two compartments. There is a lure bird in one side that is fed and watered daily; some eggs bait the other side. An inquisitive crow will land on the perch which supports a hinged lid on the baited side. The perch collapses and the lid shuts.

LOADER
When shooting with two guns, the loader passes you the loaded gun and loads the one you have just used.

LOUPING-ILL
A viral disease of animals which produces a staggering gait, often with spasmodic jumps, caused by ticks.

LURE (as in training to the lure – in coursing)
Simulated hare connected to a 150 yard length of cord which can be wound rapidly on to a drum. It is used for training greyhounds.

LURES (as in fishing)
An artificial bait resembling a small fish.

MARCH
A boundary.

MARKED
All canines urinate on things as a form of proof of ownership, or to mark territorial boundaries. Foxes will sometimes mark an animal they have killed and intend to come back for later, leaving a very distinctive smell.

MARRIAGE LINES
One's marriage certificate.

MATCH COURSING
All coursing under National Coursing Club rules. Points are awarded for various stages of the chase. The aim is not to kill the hare but to test the speed and stamina of the dogs.

MATT GRASS
A type of coarse rush grass.

MEET
A term used for the location from which hounds move off to draw (qv), the first covert (qv), often a pub.

MASTER or MFH
Master of Foxhounds.

MONOCULTURE
The cultivation of a single crop, or the maintenance of a single kind of animal, to the exclusion of others.

MOTHER UP
To suckle young; and to ensure that a young lamb, or lambs, are with their mother.

MOULT
Shed feathers.

MOUNTED
On horseback.

MUIRBURN
Scottish term for burning heather.

MYXOMATOSIS
A highly infectious viral disease of rabbits characterized by fever, and the presence of myxomata, or benign tumours containing mucous material.

NOMINATOR
A person with a right to run a dog in the Waterloo Cup. It remains a considerable honour to be elected a nominator.

OWNED THE LINE
Followed the scent without check (qv).

PACK (as in hunting)
A quantity of hounds kept for hunting.

PARR
Salmon up to two years old that are distinguishable by dark spots and transverse bands.

PEAT-HAGS
Broken peaty ground.

POACHER
A person who takes game or fish illegally.

POLDER
A piece of low-lying land reclaimed from the sea, always protected by dykes.

POOR DOERS
Any stock that loses condition, or does not look as well as the others, is a poor doer.

POULTS
Young fowl, domestic or wild.

PUPPY WALKING
Generally done by farmers, who take a hound pup after it has been weaned and bring it up for the Hunt, until it is returned to the kennels at about one year old. It enables puppies to become acclimatized to farm animals.

QUAD-BIKES
An all-terrain four-wheeled motor-bike.

RABBIT BOXES
A trap for catching rabbits.

RAKE
When hill sheep graze downhill towards valley bottoms in the morning and move to high ground in the late afternoon, it is known as their daily rake.

RAPTOR
A predatory bird.

RECCE
Short for reconnaissance.

REDDS
The shallow depression a fish makes in gravel to spawn in.

RODS
The correct term for people who fish, just as guns (qv) is the correct term for people who shoot.

RUT
The period when red deer hinds are in season: late September to the end of October. Also the act of copulation, preceded by much bellowing.

SHEBEEN
Illegal grog shop where home-made booze is sold.

SHY
An artificial hide which conceals the slipper (qv) and dogs from the hare, enabling the hare to run past it in a straight line.

SKEIN
A flock of geese when in flight.

SLIPPER
A highly skilled professional registered by the National Coursing Club, who has the responsibility of ensuring that dogs are evenly released onto a fit hare that will not initially favour either dog. At the Waterloo Cup, where huge bets are placed, the slipper has to be enormously experienced.

SLIPPING (falconry)
Releasing hawks onto quarry.

SLIPS (coursing)
The special double-headed lead which, through a quick-release mechanism, allows each pair of dogs to be loosed on equal terms. Dogs are ready to race when they are 'in slips'.

SNAPHAUNCE
A primitive form of flintlock. Developed in Holland in the mid-sixteenth century. The word is taken from 'schnapp-hahn' which means pecking cock, because the striking action of the vice that holds the flint resembles that of a pecking cock.

SOUGHS
An artificial refuge for the hare, to protect her from the dogs and the dogs from running too far. Or a deliberately created escape route.

SPLIT LITTER
An earth (qv) may become foul as cubs grow, and a vixen may seek another earth to which she will move some of her cubs.

SPOONS (as in fishing tackle)
An artificial bait in the shape of the bowl of a spoon, used in spinning or trolling.

SPY
A stalker (qv) spies when he surveys deer with his telescope.

SQUAB
A four-week-old bird which is still at the fledgling stage. It often refers to a young pigeon.

STALKER
A highly skilled professional who manages a deer forest and, during the season, guides the 'gentleman' into position for a shot. More even-tempered than a ghillie. This is explained by the fact that stalkers generally only have to put up

with one cock-up a day. A ghillie spends all day dealing with them.

STEEPLECHASING
Originally, racing from one point to another easily visible point, usually a church steeple.

STELLS
Circular stone-walled sheep shelters in which shearing, etc., was performed. They became redundant with the invention of immersion dipping for fly protection. The ruins of stells can be seen all over upland Britain.

STICKLES
Fast-flowing shallow water where it runs over pebbles.

STIRRUP-CUP
A glass of something alcoholic drunk just before the Hunt moves off. To keep out the cold and inspire confidence.

STOP-KNOT
To stop a float from moving down a fishing line.

TAINCHEL
Ancient Scottish deer drive. Herds were driven into a bog or bottle-necked glen and slaughtered. It continued into the nineteenth century before stalking became popular.

TICK
Any of various blood-sucking mites which attach themselves to the skin of dogs, cattle and other mammals, and may transmit disease.

TRACES (fishing)
A length of nylon, wire or gut that attaches a hook to the line. To stop a fish like a pike biting through the line.

TRENCHER FED
At the end of the hunting season, if the pack is dispersed amongst local farmers for the summer, they are said to be trencher fed.

TRINITY FOOT BEAGLES (TFB)
Established in 1867 by WE Currey, an assistant tutor at Trinity College, Cambridge, who brought over from his home in Ireland a pack of eighteen couple of 15-inch hounds. My father whipped-in to the TFB when he was at Cambridge before the Second World War.

TRIP
A term used for a quantity of dunlin. Also used for widgeon or teal.

TURBARY
In law, the right to common grazing, and the right to dig peat for fuel on a common, or on another person's land.

UNSIGHTED
When the dog loses sight of the hare during the run up.

WALKED UP
A traditional form of shooting, which involves walking towards and flushing game. It is the opposite of driven (qv) shooting.

WHELP
Puppy.

WHIPPED-IN
A whipper-in assists a Huntsman. He can be said to have whipped-in to so-and-so, or such-and-such a pack.

WHITE HILL
A hill that has little or no heather.

WISP
A flock of snipe in flight.

WORK
The hunting action of gun dogs, or hounds.

YELD
A hind (qv) that has not had a calf in a particular year, as distinct from barren, meaning that a hind has never had a calf.

PICTURE CREDITS

Pictures taken from the BBC series 'Clarissa and the Countryman' are copyright the BBC and gratefully acknowledged.

Other photographs are copyright as follows: